Adult Children of Divorced Parents

Making Your Marriage Work

Drs. Beverly and Tom Rodgers

Scripture quotations marked (NIV) are taken from the Holy Bible, New International Version ®. Copyright © 1973, 1978, 1984 by International Bible Society Used by permission of Zondervan Publishing House. All rights reserved.

Scripture quotations marked (TLB) are taking from The Living Bible. Copyright © 1987 by Tyndale House Publishers, Inc., Wheaton, Illinois 60189. All rights reserved.

Printed in the United States of America

Publishing services by Selah Publishing Group, LLC, Tennessee. The views expressed or implied in this work do not necessarily reflect those of Selah Publishing Group.

ISBN: 978-58930-228-0
Library of Congress Control Number: 2008911591

Contents

Introduction

It has been statistically proven that adult children of divorced parents have a high rate of divorce in their own marriages. Studies also show that they are at risk in other areas of life as well. Adult children of divorce, whom we fondly refer to as ACODPs, suffer more from depression and anxiety, have lower self-esteem, and tend to tolerate or exhibit more abuse and neglect in their relationships. These statistics have plagued Tom and me both consciously and unconsciously for years because we are adult children of divorced parents. We both came from broken homes.

We have always hated that term—broken home. It sounds so negative, so damaged. We now realize that we hated the term because it lives up to its name. After our parents' divorces we felt that not only were our families broken, but something inside of us was broken as well. Years later, when we met in college, we shared our feelings about our broken families with each other. Looking back, we realized that one of the reasons that we were attracted to each other was that we understood so much of each other's insecurity and pain, because we had experienced it in our own families.

We know firsthand about the specific problems that plague adult children of divorced parents, which contribute to their high divorce rate, problems with their self-concept, problems with their performance, and problems with their ability to do relationships successfully. The new millennium has brought a great deal of literature about the problems of ACODPs. Judith Wallerstein's book, *The Unexpected Legacy of Divorce*, is one of the main catalysts. In her research she followed a group of children from affluent Marin County, near San Francisco, whose parents were divorced. She continued to interview her subjects long into adulthood. Her findings were unexpected, thus the title of her book. She unexpectedly found that children were plagued by their parents' divorces many years after the divorce took place, even as adults with families of their own.

The finding was unexpected because the common belief of the last few decades has been that while divorce may have a negative affect on young children, when these children become adults, the negative effects will disappear. Wallerstein's case studies revealed that this was not the case. She found that children of divorced parents struggle with many difficult issues long into adulthood. Many of their issues centered on their inability to develop healthy relationships. Most of Wallerstein's subjects were consciously aware of the negative effects of their parents' divorces. But with many ACODPs the affects are often unconscious, leaving them frustrated and confused as to why they respond to certain situations in destructive or unhealthy ways.

Because we are both adult children of divorced parents, this information has a special meaning for us. We resonated with Wallerstein's case examples. They were much like our own. We have struggled with many of these issues in our marriage. As marital and family therapists, we also help many ACODPs deal with their relationship issues as well. We share their struggles and triumphs. Our goal is not to blame or shame parents who divorce, including our own. We would rather spend our energy encouraging couples to learn the skills they need to stay married for a lifetime. With the divorce rate cresting over 50 percent in recent years, this can be a difficult task.

We are not alone in our effort to support marriages. One side effect of the high divorce rate in our nation is that there are many good "promarriage" movements being formed. Marriage skills training groups are sprouting up all over the country. Promarriage legislation is being implemented at both the state and national levels. More and more couples are seeking help for their relationships from therapists, mentors, and the clergy. It seems that marriage is becoming fashionable again.

An offshoot of the marriage movement is that there are many great online resources for marriage. We receive an online newsletter from The Coalition for Marriage, Family and Couples Education. This organization sponsors the yearly Smart Marriages conference in which renowned speakers on marriage and family life present programs and ideas that strengthen marriages and families. Recently, the online newsletter was sharing a review of Judith Wallerstein's book. Since the book was published, there has been a great deal of controversy about her findings. Many thought that her research methodology was not rigorous enough. Some thought that her sample size was too small. She was criticized for using composite case examples rather than actual data. We e-mailed a letter to the CMFCE Newsletter showing our support for Dr. Wallerstein. Later the e-mail was published in the newsletter so other readers could respond. We want to share a copy of this letter with you.

With all of the public dispute about Wallerstein's research methods, we believe in the merits of her findings. My husband, Tom, and I, both children of divorce, have tried to follow her as she makes appearances with some of the skeptical talk show terrorists (we mean interviewers). We applaud her, at seventy-eight years of age, for doing something to make a mark for children. Most women her age would be playing bridge or golf. We were two children whose parents could have benefitted from her advice. The following is a story about children of divorce that might interest readers.

There is a couple we know very well who could have been participants in Wallerstein's study. The wife was a child of a very verbally and physically abusive home. It was a regular occurrence for her to see her parents go to blows with each other over issues like money, in-laws, and children. Frequently the abuse would spill over onto her, especially if she tried to stop the fighting. Even though the marital storms raged constantly in her home, the last thing she wanted was for her parents to divorce. She wanted them to get help and work things out rather than give up.

When she was five years old a terrible blow hit. Her parents announced that they were divorcing. Even though the divorce ended the daily battles, it seemed to bring on a new kind of pain. It wasn't the financial stress of having less money, though this was hard, nor the stigma of growing up in the 1950s as one of the few children living in a single-parent home. It was the loneliness and pain of realizing that the two people she loved the most could not live together, causing her family to be destroyed.

She and her siblings could have been poster children for Wallerstein's findings. Her older brother turned to drugs, her sister suffered with depression and a suicide attempt, and her lost younger brother struggled in school and with low self-esteem. By all accounts everyone would say that she faired the best through the divorce, graduating at the top of her class in high school, college, and even graduate school—busying herself with overachievement to push away the pain of her broken home. She was much like the hero, Karen, in Wallerstein's study.

It would stand to reason that marriage would be difficult for her and, in true unconscious style, she married a man whose parents were divorced as well. The two felt at home understanding each other's woundedness and empathizing with each other's plights. As expected, they have had their struggles. Both started out marriage with more than an average fear of abandonment. Both were insecure and untrusting. Both knew that they had no parental mentors, helpers, or examples of a commitment like their many friends who came from intact families. They were jealous of these friends and angry that they started their marital journey with so many handicaps that resulted from their parents' respective divorces.

The good news is that, because of their parents' divorces, and almost in spite of them, they have worked very hard to make their marriage work for the last twenty-five years. They defied the statistics that indicate that children of divorce have a higher divorce rate. By all accounts, they look like a successful couple. They have successful careers, a twenty-five-year strong marriage and two healthy, happy children. So what about them? Are they unscathed? Couldn't we use them in a study on resilience to counter Wallerstein's findings? Don't they prove what divorce supporters are saying—that kids are hearty and can do just fine after their parents divorce?

No, indeed, we could not. Because even though these two wounded souls have survived their families' disintegration for more than three decades, there is not a day that goes by, a holiday, a birthday, a special event that they do not wish that their parents could have made it work. The hollowness of having a fractured family haunts them both. Oh, they look resilient and successful, but there is no doubt in their minds that life would have been so much better if their parents had given them the legacy of a healthy intact family.

The reason we know this couple so well is because we *are* this couple. This is the story of us. We have often said that we became marriage counselors and educators to prevent children from feeling the pain we felt. It frustrates us to hear Wallerstein's opponents say that divorce will not negatively affect children; that they are strong and sturdy and can survive. From the strongest to the weakest, children suffer when their parents divorce.

When we meet couples who are contemplating terminating their marriage we want them to know about the alarming negative statistics about children of divorce. We encourage them to get all of the help they can, in hopes that they will think long and hard about their decision. We hope that by giving them cause for pause, they will do whatever they can to learn the skills to build a successful marriage, in order to spare their children some of these plights.

After writing this e-mail, we left town for several days on a speaking tour, and when we returned home, we were surprised to find at least thirty e-mails from people who read our story and wanted to respond. Many of them strongly identified with us and shared their own stories. Some expressed appreciation for our courage, honesty, and openness. This was very encouraging to us because telling our story, even years later, left us feeling somewhat vulnerable and raw. We were grateful for their support.

Some people offered dissenting views, feeling that maybe divorce is getting a bad rap, and that many of the feelings we expressed in our story could easily be attributed to other childhood issues such as violence, abuse, and poor parental communication. They argued that divorce may have even been necessary because of the violence that occurred in Bev's family. All of these points have merit. But having lived through our family struggles, it would be hard to convince us that we would not be better off in many ways if our parents had stayed married to each other. We feel passionately that much of the mistrust, fear, and insecurity we brought into our marriage came from our parents' divorces. That is not to say that adult children of other types of dysfunctional homes do not suffer from some of these same maladies. We are merely stating that we do. Just admitting that helps us. This declaration helps us clarify ourselves and motivates us to work harder on our relationship.

In *The Unexpected Legacy of Divorce* Wallerstein wrote, "Divorce may liberate parents but it traps their sons and daughters for years. It is a river they have to cross that other kids don't have. And they've got to find out how to do it. They're going to ford that river, or build a bridge over it, learn to swim or drown."

As ACODPs, our marriage was drowning and we didn't know why. We were studying to be marriage counselors, learning all the tricks of the trade, and were continually haunted by insecurities and fears that thwarted our marital contentment. Acknowledging the wounds we secretly tried to repress and attaching these wounds to the dissolution of our parents' marriages gave us insight into the dysfunctional relational patterns that haunted us as newlyweds.

We were wounded. The demise of our parents' marriages scared us in much the same way that it scares ACODPs today. In our excess baggage we drug around fear, insecurity, and anger, which led to low self-esteem, poor communication skills, and a lack of conflict resolution abilities. We had no parental role models to look to or close family mentors to guide us. We were sailing on the sea of marriage with very poor navigational skills. Just realizing this put words and reason to our pain. This language brought understanding and, with understanding, hope.

From this hope sprang an awareness that we were going to consciously combat the demons ACODPs possess. We vowed to learn skills, communication tools, and techniques to build a healthy marriage. It worked and has continued to work for the past twenty-five years. We share this not to set ourselves up as successful role models but rather to point to our many failures and attempts to pick ourselves up and paste our marriage back together, and forge ahead. We feel that if we can do it, anyone can.

Now we have the privilege of helping other struggling ACODPs navigate the vast sea of marriage. We teach them what we have learned, and as always, they teach us. This volume is dedicated to them. It will include our story, complete with marital successes and failures. We will also share real-life case examples of couples who have honored us as our clients. Their names have been changed to protect their privacy, but their messages are potent nonetheless.

Many of you may ask, "But what if your parents' divorce was actually a good thing? What if they were in constant conflict or there was violence present?" Maybe you even wanted them to end their bad marriage to keep the peace or to simply stop the pain in your home. Some of you knew that your parents were miserable and you just wanted them to end their suffering. This is true with many of the people we see in counseling. They felt that their parents' marriage was dead, and they just wanted them to bury it and get on with their lives. Some of you may be divorced yourselves and feel guilty just reading a book like this that talks about the negative effects this has had on your own children. Sometimes divorce happens even to good people, even to people who try to prevent it. The purpose of this book is not to induce guilt or to blame parents who divorce. Its purpose is to help all children of divorce understand its effects and learn to deal with these effects in a healthy way.

We do not want to debate the cause and effect of divorce, nor do we want to argue if these ill effects could have come as a result of other dysfunctions in the family system. Arguing about this is a waste of time. Learning what we can do to build strong marriages makes better sense. We simply want to point out the obvious—divorce hurts children. As a result, parents should do everything possible to become healthy and heal their marriage. Staying together and trying to work out the struggles in an unfulfilling marriage sounds like torture, but researchers Maggie Gallagher and Linda Waite reported in their book, *The Case for Marriage*, that even bad marriages improve over time. They found that 86 percent of unhappily married couples who stuck it out saw that, five years later, their marriages were happier. Their conclusion is that a bad marriage is not a fixed fact. They defined bad marriages not as those containing abuse and violence but rather those that have ordinary woes.

They found that if these marriages did not end in divorce, they actually improved over time. Just as good marriages go bad, bad marriages can go good, if you hang in there.

All married couples can benefit from learning how to communicate effectively, resolve conflict, and build intimacy, and the purpose of this book is to show every couple how. Contrary to what many people believe, even volatile couples can learn to have healthy relationships if they will learn the skills to do so. Marriage is hard work, pure and simple, and all couples can benefit from learning how to do this hard work.

Our goal in this book is to teach ACODPs how to overcome the legacy given them by their parents' divorces, to teach them how to have a healthy, successful, lasting marriage in spite of the wounds that occurred in their lives as a result of their family's dissolutions. It is to teach them how to beat the odds against them in marriage.

If you are an ACODP or are married to one, or if you just want to learn more about building a healthy marriage, read on. You will learn how to build a bridge of awareness about how your woundedness affects your marriage, how to successfully swim the channel of marital conflict, and how to ford the river of dyadic communication. As we learn from each other's mistakes and are shored up by each other's triumphs, together we as ACODPs can save each other from drowning. We can all cross Wallerstein's metaphorical river together with the hope that our destiny will be quite different from our parents'. Together we can beat the odds. God bless you in your journey to the other side.

Chapter 1

The Wounding of America through Divorce

Each year more than one million children experience the divorce of their parents. In the year 2000, more than half of all children born to married parents suffered through the divorce of their parents. Until recently the prevailing cultural attitude about children of divorce is that they will be okay. Statements abounded such as, "Children are resilient, therefore, they will survive," "Divorce is no worse for kids than living with parents who have a bad marriage," "If parents leave an unfulfilling marriage to find fulfillment elsewhere, their children will understand," "Children would not want their parents to sacrifice happiness for their sake." Researchers who have studied children of divorce are finding that this is simply not the case.

Some theorists even go so far as to say that couples should consider staying together for the sake of the children and it doesn't matter to the children if the parents are in fulfilling marriages or not. Several months ago there was an article in *The Charlotte Observer* about a couple, the Ellises, who said that the love between the two of them had died, but they agreed to stay together to raise their child in an intact family. The decision to do this caused Cheryl Ellis to go in search of other couples who were doing the same thing. She then decided to complete her doctoral dissertation on parenting partners or "parentners" as she called them. She found and interviewed several couples who had made the same choice. Some had better outcomes than others, but the Ellises were convinced that their decision to stay together in a dead marriage for their child's sake was the right decision, and they have no regrets. To quote Mrs. Ellis, "I felt that it was the ultimate sacrifice for my child, and it was worth it." Critics of this notion wonder if this is actually good for children. However, with current evidence that supports that divorce has such negative effects on children long into adulthood, this movement is getting a great deal of support.

We believe that children are resilient and survive amazing things in their lives, but even in the cases where marriages are clearly in trouble, most children want their parents to stay together so their family can remain intact. Children want the stability of a two-parent home with their original mother and original father.

Divorce causes wounds. In our book *Soul-Healing Love*, we call these wounds soul wounds, which by definition are needs from childhood which were not met and have a detrimental effect on your soul or psyche. The soul wounds caused by divorce affect the psyche in four main areas:

1. Self-esteem, which is how we feel about ourselves
2. Performance, which is how we function, grow, and adapt to life
3. Social skills, which is how we get along with peers, work, church, community, and the world at large
4. Marriage and relationships, which is how we respond with intimates

Having divorced parents can drastically affect some or all of these areas. If you are an adult child of divorce, just knowing about these wounds can be liberating. In later chapters we will help you find ways to heal these wounds. But first, let's get a better understanding of how these areas affect you.

Self-Esteem Wounds

Family is the main place from which we get our sense of connectedness and belonging. It is where our roots are established. The sense of "I am" in each of us comes from our family. Divorce dissolves families and therefore tears away at our sense of self. Our roots get shaken and our self-esteem suffers.

Depression

Thomas Parish in his 1987 study in Journal of Social Behavior and Personality, is just one of many researchers who found that divorce, and the subsequent absence of the father which often accompanies it, has been associated with diminished self-concepts in children. The sense of loss that overtakes children of divorce can create fear, insecurity, anger, and depression, which also damage self-esteem. The continual war many divorced parents wage over the affection of their children and grandchildren can further erode their self-concept. The common insults about each other that divorced parents hurl at their children can be damaging to self-esteem as well.

Anxiety

Dr. Jean Twenge from Case Western University in Cleveland found that healthy children reported more anxiety during the 1980s than child psychiatric patients reported in the 1950s. She states that children's anxiety levels strongly reflect what is happening in society at large. She believes that the social isolation caused by high divorce rates might underlie higher levels of anxiety among today's young people.

Rejection

Children often see divorce as a form of rejection. Neil Kalter, PhD, at the University of Michigan says that young girls experience the emotional loss of father egocentrically as rejection of themselves. The continued limited involvement from the father is experienced as ongoing rejection by him. Many girls attribute this rejection to not being pretty enough or smart enough to please their father and engage him in regular frequent contacts. This causes intensified separation anxiety, denial, and avoidance of feelings associated with loss of father and object hunger for males. Many of these girls lose their virginity at a younger age and have higher rates of promiscuity. Sixty-three percent showed subjective psychological problems defined as anxiety, sadness, pronounced moodiness, phobias, and depression.

Bev's Story

The rejection girls experience when their father is absent is referred to as "father hunger" or "male hunger." It can be a very unhealthy force in the life of young women if it is not realized and dealt with. This was a dilemma I faced. After my parents' divorce my father only visited about once a month. Those visits dwindled even more when he remarried and had another family to care for. I missed him terribly, especially at birthdays and holidays. There was a giant hole in my soul. It ached for a father's love, time, and attention. I was unaware of it, but it made me vulnerable to the attention of men and frightened of them at the same time.

It was during my adolescence that my father's visits really diminished. Around that time, my sister and I were selected as drum majorettes by our young, attentive, new band director. The director paid special attention to my sister and me. He said that it was because we were the only kids in the band who did not have a father to regularly watch our performances. We would baby-sit for him and work extra hours after school collecting music and grading papers. In my vulnerable state I was unaware that his motives might not be pure. I was just glad to have the attention. This allowed the young band leader to not only take advantage of my time but to take advantage of my affection as well. I was a naïve, attention starved-adolescent, and he had less than good intentions. Unfortunately, I couldn't see this.

Thank goodness his advances stopped at the point of "supportive hugs" and uncomfortable touches. He was asked to leave the school before he had the chance to harm me further. Apparently, he was being brought up on charges by a young girl at the previous school where he had worked for taking indecent liberties with her. Not surprisingly, she was the only girl in that band who had divorced parents. It seems girls like us were easy targets for this type of man. After that experience, my ability to trust was fractured even more, and I did not think I would ever trust a man again. It took several years and a lot of therapy before my suspicious nature regarding men dwindled. I even brought a trace of it into our marriage.

Health Problems

Children of divorced parents exhibit more health problems, as well as behavioral and emotional problems, than children of intact families. They are involved more frequently in drug and alcohol abuse and have higher rates of suicide. When I started my practice twenty-two years ago, there was a rash of teen suicides in Mecklenburg County, North Carolina. All but one of these teens were from broken homes. I treated quite a few adolescent children of divorce who were hopeless and despairing because their families had fallen apart.

There are also studies that point to the sense of unworthiness children of divorce feel in blended families. Last year *The New York Times* reported a study at Princeton that showed that children in families with stepmothers are likely to have less health care, less education, and less money spent on food than children raised by their biological mothers. Among children over a year old, living with both biological parents, the health study found that 61 percent have received medical checkups within the last year. But among those living with a stepmother and birth father that dropped to 46 percent.

These findings are not aimed at reincarnating the myth of the wicked stepmother. We are all aware of the difficult task of being a stepparent. But statistics clearly show that less care is being given to children of divorce who live in these situations and this could easily contribute to feelings of unworthiness and low self-esteem in children of divorce. The low self-esteem created by the plights of adult children of divorce can also affect their performance in negative ways.

Performance Wounds

Diminished Learning Capacity

Children of divorce frequently exhibit problems with their performance that can affect the rest of their lives. We have seen previously that they suffer from some serious emotional problems which can affect their performance. Research also indicates that they show diminished learning capacity, more frequent school failure, more skipping school, and lower rates of graduation from high school and college attendance than children from intact families. Because education and school performance greatly contribute to better vocational opportunities and abilities, then children of divorce are often handicapped vocationally. Their lower educational levels lead to diminished earning potential.

Lower Education Level

In Wallerstein's study of children from 131 families of divorce in Marin County, California, only two-thirds of her group went to college compared to 85 percent of the children from intact families. This lower education level for ACODPs could be attributed to the family's lower income level after the divorce. Many noncustodial parents don't follow-through with paying for college and single parents simply cannot afford it. Some researchers go so far as to say that divorce has had a greater effect on the household income of the custodial parent that the Great Depression had on the American economy decades ago.

Poor Adult Guidance

Poor performance for ACODPs can also be a result of the fact that families tend to fall apart after the divorce. No one plans for the future. Survival of the present is the primary objective. Often their parents are hurting emotionally, dating and trying to start over or working extra jobs to make ends meet after the family splits. Parents are preoccupied and the children get left out. This can be particularly damaging if the child is finishing high school and needs direction for his or her future. ACODPs tend to get less guidance in planning for college because parents stop working together for their children's future. This was also the case in my family.

More of Bev's Story

I can remember when my twin sister and I were planning for college. All of our friends' parents were writing to local universities, taking trips, and checking on loans and scholarships. My friends had confidence in their parents' wisdom and guidance. They seemed sure of what they wanted and where they wanted to go. I felt like I had no one to guide me. Whenever I asked one of my parents for help, they sent me to the other. I hoped that they could come to some kind of agreement on ways to help us. But they could not stand to be in the same room, much less to discuss sharing financial responsibility for our college education. Even though my sister and I graduated at the top of our class we still had a deep fear that we were not going to get a college education. If it had not been for the help of our interested saintly minister and his wife we would not have received the aid we needed.

How I envied my friends from intact families. They seemed to make decisions with ease, get married with relative assurance of success, and select careers with a quiet confidence. I had none of that because what rumbled beneath my performance-oriented, perfectionistic exterior was a frightened insecure little girl who wondered if she would ever make it in life and how that was going to happen. I hated those years of fear and anxiety and have no doubt that much of that came from my parents' divorce and their inability to deal with each other with civility afterward.

I started writing books when I was forty-two years old. I wanted to write years earlier, but what held me back was a deep-seated feeling that my performance would be substandard and no one would want to hear what I had to say. While there were other factors playing a part in my insecurities, you will never convince me that these feelings were not exacerbated by the dissolution of my family. I am sure that I would have started writing a decade earlier and would also be living a life with much more confidence and much less fear had my parents given me the precious legacy of an intact family.

Societal Wounds

Because divorce damages self-esteem as well as performance, it stands to reason that it wounds society as well. It has significant economic consequences for society because it translates into fewer family members receiving college educations. This causes reduced earning potential among family members and a higher risk of poverty, all of which can be detrimental to our social structure.

Criminality

Perhaps one of the greatest effects of divorce on society is the devastating correlation between divorce and crime. Robert Sampson, from the University of Chicago, studied 171 U.S. cities with populations of more than 100,000 and found that lower rates of divorce yielded lower rates of crime. One study from the University of Wisconsin found that the rates of incarceration for adult children of divorced parents were twelve times higher than their counterparts from intact families.

Children of divorce are more likely to become delinquent by the age of fifteen, and divorce of parents before a child reaches age ten is a major predictor of adolescent delinquency and adult criminality. Because divorce increases feelings of rejection and hostility in children it can increase their vulnerability for gang involvement in our urban communities. A review of literature revealed that divorce increases the likelihood that a child will abuse drugs and alcohol, especially if the divorce occurs during the adolescent years. Alcohol and drug abuse have been linked to all types of criminal behavior. A national longitudinal study tracked boys over a twenty-year period and found that those without biological fathers in the home were three times more likely to commit crimes that led to incarceration.

Abuse and Neglect

Divorce is a relevant factor in child abuse. High levels of divorce accompany high levels of child abuse, and remarriage does not reduce the level of child abuse, and may even increase it. Studies show that serious abuse is more likely to occur with stepchildren than with children of intact families. The rate of sexual abuse among stepdaughters is six times higher than daughters of biological fathers.

Religious Life

Divorce weakens the religious life of a family. Often the families that worshiped together do not continue this practice after the divorce. Because religious worship is linked to better health and happiness and stronger values, this can have a negative effect on society. When a family falls apart, the members lose faith in God and even faith in life.

One newly married young man told us that he had prayed for years that his parents would resolve their differences and stay together. After his parents' divorce he quit praying and never resumed the practice. He came to counseling with his new bride because she wanted him to attend church with her and he was skeptical and resistant. This is only one of many ACODPs we have treated who have a difficult time finding their faith after their parents' divorces.

These negative effects of divorce disintegrate the structure of the family, which is the building block of society. Therefore, divorce puts society at risk. Patrick Fagan and Robert Rector, directors of The Heritage Foundation, a national organization that does research on aspects of marriage and family life, have spent years collecting data on children of divorce. They say that if nothing is done about the climbing divorce rate in our country, then America will continue on a downward spiral into social decay. They challenge policy makers at the federal and state levels to change the current culture of divorce. They encourage them to expand marriage education and promote divorce prevention programs. It seems that the powers that be are listening, and changes are taking place, but there is still so much that has to be done to heal the wounds divorce has inflicted on society as a whole.

Relationship Wounds

Research shows that adult children of divorced parents have a difficult time forming intimate relationships. We speak on relationships across the country. One of our favorite venues is to speak about our book *How to Find Mr. or Ms. Right* on college and university campuses. We teach college students how to seek out a healthy mate and become one themselves.

So many of these young people are children of the boomer generation and come from divorced homes. They lament that they are fearful of getting married because they are concerned that their marriage won't last. They don't know how to resolve conflict or communicate effectively because they never saw their parents do this successfully. This feeling is exacerbated by the statistical proof that they are at a high risk for divorce.

We tell our audiences that ACODPs are relationally challenged. This is the politically correct way of saying that they will have trouble forming healthy intimate relationships. Because of this, they need to address the issues from their parents' divorces. There are many reasons for the relational maladies of the ACODP. One is their lack of trust in themselves and others. We will spend a whole chapter on this subject, but in a nutshell, relationships are built on trust. Because of their real or perceived rejection and abandonment, trust can be very difficult for them. Add to that the fear that they might be abandoned by their partner, and you can see why trust will be problematic for them.

No Role Models

Often ACODPs have trouble in relationships because they do not have good relationship role models. They watched as their parents did not resolve conflict in a healthy way and they fear that they will follow in their parents' footsteps. When a child looks on as the love between his parents turns to contempt, he or she can feel inferior at developing healthy relationships. While adult children of intact families can have trouble resolving conflict, ACODPs do not have the privilege of seeing arguments resolved by happy marital partners. Wallerstein likens it to being a dancer without ever having seen a dance.

The Story of Us

The lack of healthy marital role models caused us a great deal of fear when we were contemplating marriage. We knew we were deeply in love and that the chemistry between us was great, but we had a great deal of difficulty resolving conflict. The way I adapted to the woundedness of my parents' divorce was to be a pleaser, a fixer. I believe the term is codependent! If there was a problem, I would try to achieve peace at any price. My greatest fear was being abandoned, so I did whatever I could to prevent this, often giving in when I needed to set a firmer boundary.

Tom, on the other hand, adapted to his parents' divorce by withdrawing from his family. He distanced himself by staying busy with sports and school. He became a loner. His conflict resolution style was to blow up and then withdraw and be alone. As you can see, we had very opposite styles of conflict resolution. This is often the case, that people with similar wounds are attracted to one other. Unfortunately, they have opposite adaptations to those wounds. While it is true that opposites do attract, they also conflict about the very issues that attracted them in the first place. Opposites attract, even in conflict.

When we first met, our opposing styles were attractive to one another. But as time went on, the very style that attracted us became a huge stumbling block. Our opposing styles were detrimental for each other and our marriage. It is no wonder that we sought marital therapy when we had only been married six months.

We have dedicated an entire chapter to how we learned to resolve conflict in a healthy manner. You can read more about this later. There are still other ways in which ACODPs have unhealthy relationships. In order to heal them, it is necessary to be aware of what they are.

ACODPs As Victims

Children of divorce are more frequently victims of abuse and neglect than their counterparts from intact families. Because of these and other childhood wounds, they are more likely to be in abusive relationships or become abusive themselves. They live what they learn, and they have grown comfortable or familiar with this type of dysfunction. So many violent couples come from homes where violence was present. It takes a lot of hard work to teach them that there is a better way to relate than what they learned from their family-of-origin.

Conclusion

This data clearly shows us that children of divorce suffer from specific soul wounds. These wounds follow them into adulthood, causing them to be at risk in marriage. They have low self-esteem, insecurity, and fear of rejection and abandonment. They suffer from emotional problems such as depression and anxiety, which often lead them to abuse alcohol and drugs. To add to this, adult children of divorced parents tend to handle marital conflict in destructive ways, often enduring or inflicting more abuse and neglect in relationships than adult children from intact families. With all of these struggles you can see why adult children of divorce are at a higher risk for divorce themselves.

ACODPs often carry with them an insecurity that the relationship will not last. This sense of doom haunts them. One woman said that during her teen years her parents would threaten divorce and ask her to choose whom she would live with. She said that she felt a cloud of doom hanging over her after that. Her parents finally split and she went into a deep depression. As a young married woman she just couldn't shake this feeling that the proverbial shoe would drop and misery would come crashing down on her again. This caused her a great deal of difficulty in her marriage.

The lack of healthy marital role models handicaps ACODPs as well. They have no reference for healthy conflict resolution. In their family, the only solution was dissolution. They do not have the support of intact parents who have weathered the storms of a long healthy marriage. This was the case with us. During the first year of marriage, when we would have difficulty resolving conflict, we couldn't imagine calling our parents for help. At that point, Tom's dad was on his third marriage and we felt his track record indicated that he would be of little assistance. We craved mentors to teach us the ropes.

Feelings of self-blame, impotence, shame, and powerlessness haunt ACODPs. They wish that they could have done something to prevent the dissolution of their family. This can lead to them taking too much responsibility in their marriage and risk becoming codependent or too little responsibility and becoming disengaged. After their parents divorce many children "check out" of life emotionally. When they are courting their spouse this disengagement does not surface. But as time progresses and the honeymoon effect fades, they return to what is familiar to them—the old comfortable distancing pattern.

Loyalty issues haunt adult children of divorced parents as they try to make sense of their extended family and try to maintain family ties. They feel torn and divided on special events, holidays, and family vacations. Divorce fractures families so much that many ACODPs just stop participating in family gatherings and reunions. It becomes too painful and difficult for them. If parents put kids in the middle, then they will struggle with guilt as they spend time with one parent and not the other. If the parents can't stand each other, which is often the case, the adult child is forced to make a choice as to who to invite to special events. This leaves one parent out and creates even more guilt and frustration for the adult child.

Our parents were like this. They could not get along. They did not speak to each other after their divorces for many years. This forced us to choose which parent to invite to special events and family functions. We were even forced to choose who to invite to our wedding. Tom's dad did not attend, nor did my mother. What a choice to make for a young bride and groom!

Recently, we worked with an engaged couple who were both ACODPs. As they were planning their wedding, the bride's mom and dad became jealous of each other's contributions to their daughter's wedding. They began to bribe their daughter with money to ignore the advice of the other parent. It was as if they were paying for her loyalty through offering to pay for her wedding. As if this was not bad enough, the groom's father refused to let the groom's mother and her husband participate in the rehearsal dinner if he was paying for it! Here was this young beautiful couple, full of excitement and hope, very much in love and wanting to start a life together, having to wade through the muck and mire of their immature, selfish parents. It should not have to be this way. The lack of intact families-of-origin puts stress on marriages. With families sinking all around them, it can be difficult for them to stay afloat.

Can ACODPs Beat the Odds?

One of the most common questions we get asked is, "Do we think that completion and healing is possible for adult children of divorced parents? Can they live healthy productive lives, and have successful relationships?" Our answer is an unequivocal *yes*, but not without very hard work. The hard work comes with the awareness that you are wounded and that these wounds negatively affect your marriage. You will need to learn the skills of healthy couples and practice them. This book is designed to make this task easier for you.

As you heal, there will be scars left on your soul to remind you of your journey. This is true for us. There are situations in life that kindle thoughts of what could have been. We still hate explaining to our children why they have four sets of grandparents. We struggle with the confusion on their innocent faces when they try to figure out how they are related to some obscure steprelative. It hurts us that we can never be together as a family and how siblings have grown distant and detached from family gatherings, which is a common side effect of having divorced parents.

These scars have a positive side, however. Because of the pain we suffered twenty-five years ago, we entered into marriage with a resolve that we would not divorce. There was no back door for us. We said that we would never put our children through this. Suffering through our parents' bitter, painful divorces inspired us to do the hard work to make our marriage last. We were conscious that fear, insecurity, and anxiety would rear their ugly heads in our relationship and we combated them with awareness, communication, intentionality, relationships skills training, commitment, and a whole lot of prayer.

We will always wish that marriage did not have to be so hard for us. We watched our friends from intact families sail through issues that caused us to struggle for days. Now two and a half decades later, we realize that good came from our struggles. We learned specific skills and developed our own tools and communication techniques because of our marital dilemmas. We are now able to impart them to other ACODPs so that their struggles can be eased.

In the next few chapters you will see how to become aware of soul wounds such as trust, fear, and insecurity. You will learn tools that are designed to heal the soul wounds of adult children of divorced parents. We will share communication techniques designed to bring about sharing, understanding, and empathy.

Salted throughout this book are stories of our own wounds as ACODPs and how we achieved healing. Our vulnerability is not easy at times, but it is worth it to us to forge a trail for you, the reader, and other ACODPs who, after reading, will have a compass to navigate the frightening yet wonderful journey called marriage.

Chapter 2

Awareness: Bev's Story

The statistics in the previous chapter are disturbing for many people. While it is true that these findings may not apply to all ACODPs, the effects of divorce are indeed grim. Many adult children of divorced parents want to deny this. They think that if they become aware of the ill effects of divorce on their life, then they are somehow defective. Others think that looking at the negative effects of their parents' divorces is somehow blaming their parents or saying that their parents are bad people.

By looking at your parents' divorce, you are not blaming them or shaming them, you are merely gaining insight about yourself. It helps you learn what motivates you to act the way you do. Many parents did the best they could. They had fewer resources to aid in marriage than exist today. The most obvious conclusion that we can draw from the data in the previous chapter is that today's parents should strongly consider all options before divorcing in order to prevent any of the negative effects of divorce from plaguing their children.

That being said, we do not advocate blaming our parents or holding them as emotional hostages for our current marital problems either. Rather, we promote enabling ourselves to gain insight and awareness into our own behavior. If we are not aware of how our parents' divorces affected us, then we will be unaware of many of the destructive patterns that we have developed in our own marriages. Thus, we will be unable to repair these dysfunctional patterns. In order to look forward, we must first look back.

Looking Back

For some of you this look back can be painful. That is why you have avoided this journey. This pain is necessary to get you to go where you need to go. The adage, "You can't heal what you can't feel" is applicable. Some of you don't want to look back because you think this is wallowing in self-pity. It is only self-pity if you don't grow from it.

Some of you don't want to look back because you are perennial optimists, and looking back is too pessimistic for you. You will be surprised at how taking this journey back is more positive than you think. Our journey into the past was painful, but insightful, and had very positive results.

The Story of Us

We started our marriage with all of the naiveté and hubris a young couple could possess. To add to our false pride, I was studying to be a marital and family therapist and Tom was studying religion. Of course, we thought that the study of such noble pursuits would inoculate us against any ill effects of our parents' marital failures. With all of our wisdom and knowledge, we thought that we could glide through marriage with a minimal amount of problems. It did not take long for us to realize that wisdom and knowledge could not immunize us against the marital maladies that marred us as ACODPs.

If knowledge wasn't enough, we thought that a shared religious faith might be the vaccination from struggle that our marriage needed. Our faith gave us a higher purpose and goal to stay together. While it was helpful, it did not prevent us from being stricken with many relational maladies. We thought our faith was helpful, but other couples weren't so fortunate, and with the divorce rate for religious couples cresting at 57 percent, it became apparent to us that faith is not always a salve for marital wounds. In order to show you what helped two hopeless ACODPs build a healthy happy marriage, perhaps we need to start at the beginning.

Bev's Beginning

I grew up in the Deep South, the second born of four children. My brother was two years older; my twin sister was only two minutes younger, and I had a baby brother who was six years my junior. My father was an insurance salesman and my mother was a homemaker. My mother stayed at home during my early years. I actually have a few early childhood memories of delicious home cooked meals around the table. That all began to fall apart when I was around four-years-old. My parents' constant fighting began to tarnish those shiny memories. I don't remember what they fought about, but I do remember the fights. My mother was a very angry person and would become irate and out of control very easily. Often, her anger turned into physical abuse and she would attack my father, who would defend himself by blocking her punches or getting out of her way.

These violent episodes increased as I grew older. It seemed money, jealousy, and suspicion of other women fueled mom's fire toward my dad. Mom even broke a bottle over his head once. I can still see the blood streaming down his neck and chest. This kind of trauma stays with a child for quite a while.

When I speak to audiences on developing healthy relationships, I share about my childhood. I tell audiences that my parents had what I call "redneck fights" when I was growing up. Since they both were reared in the hills of Tennessee, this description seemed appropriate. I define redneck fights as watching an episode of the television show, *Cops*, only without the cops! In a typical episode of this show there were usually two incoherent adults hurling obscenities, as well as fists, at each other. The sound of flesh is grinding in the background. There are several pitiful, ill clad, terrified children huddled together in the corner. The children are crying and begging the adults to stop fighting. Thus were the pathetic scenes from my childhood.

When I was five years old, my parents had a particularly violent redneck fight. That evening my mother hurled insults and accusations at my father who frantically announced that he had had enough of my mother's craziness and that he was leaving. As I heard this, my short life passed before my eyes. I panicked. "Leave," I cried, "You can't leave! What will we do? How will we survive?" I grabbed his leg and begged him to stay. He literally dragged me across the plank floor of our little house, opened the screen door and flung me off of his leg. I can still feel the pain of pressing my face against the screen door, and begging him to come back. All I could think about was, "Who will take care of us? Will we be all right?" Even at age five I knew that my mother had serious problems and that my father's exit would be fatal to my family. I knew my mom was incapable of caring for us.

My dad did leave, and life was bleak. Without his income, our family's socioeconomic status took a huge nosedive. His limited child support was not enough to support four children. Because of my mom's inadequate education, the only job she could get was as a waitress in a local hotel. She worked as a waitress during the day and substituted as bartender when they needed her.

Needless to say, family dinners ended. I became a little adult almost overnight. I would come home from school, help my mother get her uniform pressed and ready, polish her shoes, and get her off to work. My sister and I would then prepare dinner. Our young culinary abilities were limited so our nightly delicacies typically consisted of fish sticks and beanie weenies. To this day, I won't eat either!

Since we had little money, there were no more vacations, no more family trips, no more laughter around the table, and no more special treats after dinner. It seemed our family just survived. Something vibrant had died. We were parentless, latchkey waifs who were left to sail on the sea of the turbulent '60s. This antiestablishment mentality of the time was the perfect place for my older brother to put his hostility and anger. He was a brilliant student until my dad left. After my parents' divorce, he became the classic underachiever. He started cutting class, skipping school, and eventually failing a grade. The hippie drug culture absorbed him, and like many others, he started medicating his pain by using alcohol and drugs. He smoked pot, dropped acid, and drank with a destructive vengeance. He acted out his hostility by getting in fights, theft, and other delinquent behavior. Eventually, he dropped out of school and ran away from home to live in a commune. There were months when we did not even see him or know if he was alive or dead. He was truly a causality of my parents' divorce, mirroring many of the characteristics we discussed in the previous chapter. So much of his potential was wasted because of what had happened in my family.

My dad tried to visit us regularly, but for his young daughter who adored him, the visits just were not frequent enough. Shortly after the divorce, my dad remarried a woman twenty years his junior and adopted her little girl. After that, his visits grew even more infrequent. Later, I learned that this is typical for many divorced noncustodial fathers.

Living without my dad in the home was detrimental for me. It wasn't that we were terribly close or that he was even really involved in my life. Neither of these scenarios were particularly true. I just missed him. This longing grew as I grew. I, like the girls in the study in Chapter 1, took my father's leaving as rejection. I tried to be the perfect child by making straight As, becoming a leader in school and church, and caring for my other siblings. I unconsciously thought that if I was good enough, I would get more of his time and attention. This created a great deal of "father hunger" in me.

By the time I was thirteen years old and approaching puberty, I was desperate for a boyfriend. My "father hunger" manifested itself as "male hunger" and I seemed to gravitate to guys who would fill that void by paying a lot of attention to me. The reason they were so attentive is because they were very needy. I attracted wounded guys and I felt obligated to fix them. It made me feel needed and special and took away some of the pain of my "father hunger." I thought that if they needed me to fix them, then they wouldn't abandon me. I picked emotionally and physically unavailable men. My relationships with guys replicated my relationship with my father. I was held hostage by my "male hunger" and was totally unaware of it.

With my father gone, my mother deteriorated. She began to drink and take prescription medication. She became more and more mentally unstable, and more and more abusive. I became the object of her rage. This caused me terrific shame. For years I blamed myself for attracting her wrath. It wasn't until I was in graduate school that I learned that abusive parents tend to single out one child to abuse more regularly. Usually that child is most like the absent father. Another reason I was a common target for her was because I would actually try to reason with her and calm her down. This infuriated her. She said I was talking back to her and being disrespectful.

I believe my mother's beatings were not as damaging as her verbal assaults, particularly those against my father. She could not say one positive thing about him. She regularly attacked his personality, lifestyle, and character. She would say destructive things to me such as, "Your father left you because he found another family that he liked better." I was an innocent child, and I believed her. I now realize that it was just her attempt to make my father look bad in my eyes. But the effects were devastating, nonetheless.

During my teen years, my father's visits dwindled even more. My mother hated my stepmother, so we were not allowed to visit him at his house. As a result of this my relationship with my father consisted of a few brief phone conversations each month. I poured myself into marching band, school, and my small neighborhood church. As I shared earlier, my "father hunger" created vulnerability in me which allowed me to be used by my bandleader. Fortunately, I was saved from some really horrible abuse. The support of several elderly couples in our neighborhood church eased me through my teen years. They loved and supported me, often bringing food and money to our family, and sponsoring me and my siblings on special trips. Their support sustained me through some very rough times. Later they enabled my sister and I to get full scholarships to a wonderful university in Los Angeles. I will be forever grateful to this little congregation for their kindness to me.

When I was a senior in high school, my mother's violent outbursts were more frequent and severe. Her mood was unstable and her behavior unpredictable most of the time. I would walk on eggshells whenever she was home. Frequently, she would threaten to run away and leave us or tell us that she was going to ship us off to our father. During one particularly violent episode she told me to call my father and tell him to come and get us. I mustered up all of the courage I could and called my father and asked if we could come to live with him. She got furious at me for calling, even though she was the one that told me to. This triggered her rage, and in a scene that could only be described as surreal or demonic, she started beating me uncontrollably. She threatened to kill me by stabbing me with a pair of scissors. I was immobilized with fear, so frightened that I could not even speak. My sister and brother were too frightened to help me. They just stood there frozen in shock and disbelief. All I could do was pray!

I do not know who called the police. I think it was one of our neighbors. The pounding of two uniformed officers at the front door broke my mother's concentration. As she went to the front door, we ran to the back. We narrowly escaped, taking only a few belongings and the clothes on our backs. My dad appeared in the chaos and confusion and took us away from the house we had lived in all our lives.

The adjustment to my father's house was tough for me. He and my new family tried to make us feel as welcome as possible, but the trauma of the previous events haunted me. We lived there for several peaceful, pleasant months that I desperately needed to heal. My mother's rage did not subside and she refused to speak to me, and forbade me to ever come home again. I had been uprooted from my home, placed in a strange place with a new family, and was suffering from severe rejection and post traumatic stress disorder. Six months later, I moved across the country to go to college in California.

All of this stress took a toll on my self-concept. I began college very shaky and insecure, but I hid it under my overachieving exterior. I majored in psychology which helped me a lot. I learned a great deal about my dysfunctional family and how it affected me. The four years at the college did a great deal to build my confidence in my abilities and rebuild my sense of worth.

My senior year of college, I met a handsome Californian and fell in love. We would talk into the wee hours in the morning about our hopes and dreams and would often share our childhood stories. We felt a bond, a kinship. In some ways I felt like I had known him all of my life. His childhood may not have been as traumatic as mine, but he had his share of pain from his parents' divorce as well. You will hear more about Tom's story in the next chapter.

Telling our stories is indeed difficult. As we were writing these first few chapters, we had to pause and let the emotion come. We have done a great deal of work to deal with our parents' divorces, but there is still a lingering pain and sadness about what could have been. This is not the first time we have shared the narrative of our parents' divorces with others, but each time we do it, it brings new awareness. It is tough, but we have learned that it is a path to knowledge of how our parents' divorces affected us, and this understanding can bring healing. We know that in order to be healthy we had to become aware.

EXERCISE: MY PARENTS' DIVORCE SAGA

Write a brief narrative about the circumstances of your parents' divorce. You may use Bev's story as an example. Include pertinent details that help you become aware of how their divorce impacted you. For those of you who were too young to have actual memories of your parents' divorce, you may write about what you heard from family folklore or the subsequent effects of the divorce on your life, such as living with stepparents or early memories of visitation with your noncustodial parent.

Writing your story may evoke pain. Dealing with this pain may not be easy for some of you, but if you continue the journey, through the storms of pain you can sail more wisely and peacefully on the sea of marriage. We knew that in order to be healthy we had to face our pain. This next chapter tells Tom's story and shows you how to face yours.

Chapter 3

Dealing with Pain: Tom's Story

The first twelve years of my life were very normal. We were a standard American family with a middle-class home, two kids, and a dog. We took yearly vacations and had fun like most families. My parents were very much involved in our church, with my mom teaching Sunday school, and my father serving on the church board. To me, my dad was larger than life. He was a strong, handsome, charismatic leader and I idolized him. Mom was loving and kind, and spent most of my early years as a housewife, cooking and cleaning and caring for me and my sister who was three years younger. During those years I felt safe and secure. I flourished as an athlete and student and won several awards for my musical ability.

When I was thirteen years old all of the security and stability of my loving home came crashing down when I overheard my father having a phone conversation with a woman with whom he was having an affair. I could hardly believe my ears. My father, whom I deeply loved, respected, and admired, was cheating on my mother. The feelings I had at that moment were mixed. A part of me wanted to listen in curiosity, as one would watch a horror movie, wondering what would happen next. Another part felt sickened. I listened intently until he told her he loved her. I couldn't take any more. I hung up the phone and went in my father's room to confront him. He made the mistake of trying to lie to me, telling me that I was confused about what I had heard. As I countered his defense, he then switched tracks and tried to collude me into keeping his secret. He begged me not to tell my mom, saying that it would just upset her. I knew that I could not keep a secret like this, and it was terribly unfair for him to ask me to. When my mother and sister returned home,

I told them the ugly secret. Needless to say, she became distraught and started to yell at my dad. My sister began to cry and I sat there in utter disbelief and despair.

Mom and dad began to argue and dad emerged from the room and started attacking me for telling the secret. He was furious with me, blaming me for this conflict. I was sickened with guilt and shame. I thought it was indeed my fault that their marriage was in trouble. Even after this big blowup they did not separate. My dad, however, did not speak to me for two months. This crushed me.

In a few weeks the affair became known all over our tiny central California community. We were forced to leave our home in disgrace. I will never forget the day that I had to check out of my junior high school. I had always been a good student, particularly in math. I had an excellent math teacher who really believed in me and thought that I would go far in the field. As I handed him my withdrawal form, tears filled my eyes. He knew that I was hurting, so he walked me out of the classroom, put his hands on my shoulders, and tried to encourage me. He told me that I had a very high aptitude for math and wished me success in life. I thanked him for the encouragement, but he knew intuitively that part of me had already given up. We moved back to the town where I was born, and I had to start high school without knowing a soul.

At the new high school I discovered football which became a good outlet for me. From that point on, my grades began to suffer. I learned that long-term success and planning were painful because things do not always work out the way you desire or plan. Believing that nothing would work out right anyway, I began to settle for what felt good at the moment. My spiritual faith dwindled and our family's spiritual life faded. I distrusted everyone. As my father and I grew more distant, my mother began to confide in me. It felt a lot like she was clinging to me, telling me what a bad guy my father was. I became her emotional confidant. She would tell me seemingly endless stories about my father's infidelities. I quickly learned that my role was not to try to make things better; I was just to listen and commiserate with her about what a rotten guy my father was. I actually encouraged her to leave him, but she felt that she could not make it alone with two kids. I did not want their marriage to end, but I wanted to stop the pain for all of us. Gradually, we all began to live lives of quiet desperation. I wanted so badly for them to get help, but my mother said that my father refused to go. Without help, I knew that their relationship was doomed. It was just a matter of time. I internalized a basic fear that no matter how hard you try, nothing works out in the long run. The year I graduated from college, they finally divorced, burying their dead marriage.

I managed to graduate high school and college with some renewed sense of hope. Successfully completing my education enhanced my flailing self-esteem. In college, I rediscovered my faith and grew a great deal spiritually. My hometown pastor became a mentor to me and helped me restore my faith in God, life, and marriage. My spiritual strength helped me through the final demise of my parents' marriage. Even though my faith was growing and my self-esteem improving, I was still untrusting in relationships with women.

I had a series of unhealthy relationships, including a one-year engagement that ended poorly. My relationship failures only fed my belief that things do not ultimately work out well. At times, I felt like I was destined to be alone. Then, two years after I graduated from college, I went to graduate school in Los Angeles. The first month I was there I met a vibrant, irresistible young woman from the hills of Tennessee. With Bev, I began to feel a sense of hope and optimism about relationships. She was warm and open and at times threatening, but steadfastly cared for me and seemed to invite me to share the pain that was locked within my soul. This both delighted and terrified me.

We fell in love and planned our wedding, hoping that the combination of deep devotion for each other, faith, and education would be enough to ward off most marital struggles. Little did I know that the wounds and scars of my parents' poor relationship skills and subsequent divorce would return to haunt me. Early in our marriage I was overwhelmed by a sense of doom. Even when we had little disagreements, I feared that our marriage would not survive. I remember being so afraid when Bev and I would have an argument that we were going to get a divorce. In my fear, I actually ushered this into existence by creating my own self-fulfilling prophecy. When Bev and I would argue, I would say unhealthy things like, "Why don't you just leave?" or "Let's just split if you do not like what I do." I now realize that I was unconsciously rejecting her before she could get a chance to reject me. Consequently, we were unable to resolve even minor disagreements.

I had no point of reference in resolving conflict because I never saw my parents resolve theirs. I felt like I had been called to play football and I could not read the playbook. I felt lost, frustrated, and out of place. I turned to my old pastor for help, but by then we were living far away. In researching this book, I found that other ACODPs also feel lost when it comes to knowing how to resolve conflict.

My self-concept took such a beating in childhood that it was difficult for me to feel like a worthy partner for Bev, especially in the area of sharing my thoughts and feelings. It was hard for me to express myself. I was consumed with self-doubt, particularly during marital conflicts. I would blow up and defend myself, and then shut down. Even with all of the knowledge I had, I could not seem to stop these bad relationship patterns.

Awareness Is Key

Because of our childhood wounds, we were both relating to each other in very unhealthy ways. I would become angry at a situation, then feel frustrated and impotent to share or resolve the conflict. I would then withdraw. Bev would fear abandonment and panic, which would cause her to cling to me. This created a very unhealthy pursuer/distancer dyad.

We call this dysfunctional marital pattern "Marital Pac Man," which is much like the old video game *Pac Man*, in which one player is running from the large Pac Man who is chasing him in order to swallow him. In the pursuer/distancer dyad, or the Marital Pac Man scenario, one mate runs from the other in fear that they will be chomped up. Tom's hopelessness caused him to distance himself and my fear caused me to cling, all the while whining and unsuccessfully coercing him to connect to me. The more I would pursue, the more he would distance himself. We both would become critical of each other, which only exacerbated our problems. We would end up in a hole that we could not get out of. This led us to explore why we responded the way we did in conflict.

Since I was a graduate student in marital and family therapy, the logical place for us to look for help was a family therapist. One of the first things the therapist did was to ask us questions about our families-of-origin, this being the fancy therapy term for the family that we grew up in. As he was asking these questions, we both could feel ourselves getting anxious. We thought that we had forgiven our parents, and had put all of the pain of the past behind us. We felt terribly uneasy about looking at it again. We would have done anything—read more books, taken more classes, sat through boring lectures, anything but feel our pain.

Like many other adult children of divorced parents, we tried all kinds of ways to defend against feeling our childhood hurt. We made excuses for my parents. We saw the "silver lining" in the dark clouds. We rationalized that they were better off, that at least the conflict had stopped. While these attitudes were not all bad, they were allowing us to cover up our pain. We said things like, "Why dig up the past? Why cry over spilled milk? It's done. Just make the best of it." All the while, our marriage was suffering because of our dysfunctional patterns. We were not alone in our resistance. Many ACODPs do not want to relive the feelings about their parents' divorces because they do not want to feel the pain.

Dealing with Pain

Some ACODPs have little awareness of the pain that is lurking beneath their controlled exterior. This means that a great deal of their experiences, feelings, and reactions are acted out in relationships, without their conscious awareness. When you are reacting a certain way to your spouse, and you have no clue why, it may be an unconscious reaction to the pain you do not want to feel.

As we started feeling the pain of our parents' divorces, we discovered something surprising. We learned that pain could be positive. It can even be a wise teacher that illuminates the soul. We learned that pain was not the real problem. It was our inability to deal with pain that was causing us trouble. In our book *Soul-Healing Love,* we say that we are given pain as a signal to our psyches, as well as our bodies, of danger. When we get hurt, pain is a signal that we need healing. Our pain actually signaled us where to look in determining our unhealthy relational patterns. One of the greatest difficulties in diagnosing diseases like cancer or AIDS is that people can be completely unaware that they are sick because they do not feel pain.

We have learned to see pain as a positive force, but in our western culture, pain is still negative and to be avoided at all costs. So many other cultures see suffering as a rite of passage. Some African tribes require members to endure pain and suffering to achieve manhood. Americans are a group of pleasure seekers. We want fast-acting pain relievers, quick cures for headaches, and rapid surgical options that bring a full and complete recovery, in record time. There was a popular song in the 1970s entitled, "I Haven't Got Time for the Pain." That song says it all.

Western couples want to live happily-ever-after. They don't want to hear that marriage is hard work, especially if you have divorced parents. They want to hear about wonderful couples who have happy endings with no muss or fuss. They want marital enrichment, not crisis intervention. This was brought home to us several years ago when we were asked to speak to a group of couples at a large affluent church in our community. The leaders, a couple, we will call the Smiths, were the ones that made all of the arrangements for us to come. Mr. Smith knew that we were marriage counselors and therefore treated mostly troubled couples, so he made a point of telling us several times that his group did not want to hear about depressing things like adult children of divorce, soul wounds, and childhood pain. They wanted to hear how healthy couples lived, how to make good marriages even better. We thought he was making his point a little too strongly, but we obliged him. A year later we were asked to come back and share with the group again, but the Smiths were not there. When we asked where they were, we were told that they had separated and were no longer going to that church.

Our frustration was that, of all the couples we have spoken to over the years that needed to hear about pain and childhood wounds, this was surely one. The problem was that they did not want to face their pain. The Smiths both came from divorced homes. We were saddened, but not surprised, at their plight.

The divorce of our parents causes pain. It changes the way we live. We have to make accommodations for these changes as we grow and live our lives. It greatly helps ACODPs to become aware of what this pain is about, how they adapt to it, and how it affects their marriage. The next exercise is designed to help couples do this.

EXERCISE: THE ACODP QUESTIONNAIRE

Answer each of these questions as thoroughly as possible and share the answers with your spouse.

1. How old were you when your parents divorced?
2. Did you have any idea that this was going to happen?
3. Did they tell you that they were going to divorce?
4. If they told you, what did they say?
5. How did it feel when you first heard?
6. What about your life changed at that time?
7. How has their divorce affected your life?
8. Do you ever fear that your marriage will end in divorce?
9. In your marriage, do you struggle with the following issues?

- Trust issues
  Are you concerned that your marriage will not last or that your partner will be unfaithful?

- Fear issues
  Do you fear doom, that bad things will happen when you least expect it?
  Do you have a fear of abandonment?
  Do you have a fear of failure?

- Insecurity issues
  Do you try to control every thing?
  Do you have to always be right?
  Do you have trouble taking blame or responsibility for the part you play in conflict?
  Are you too dependent and just want to be taken care of?

- Communication issues:
  Do you have difficulty expressing yourself?
  Do you have trouble being a good listener?
  Do you have trouble resolving conflict?

- Life issues
  Do you feel lost, like you don't know the ropes in marriage?
  Do you and your spouse have difficulties with in-laws?
  Do you crave mentors for marriage to show you the way?

Addressing these questions and facing the pain associated with answering them will lead you to a deeper awareness of the effects of divorce on your life. And that awareness will lead you to healing the wounds of those effects.

Chapter 4

The Inability-to-Trust Wound

Trust is a key ingredient in marriage. Many adult children of divorced parents have trouble trusting. This lack of ability to trust can take on many forms. Some of you cannot trust that your marriage will last. If adultery played a part in your parents' divorce, you may have an inability to trust that your mate will be faithful to you. You might even have trouble trusting yourself and fear that you will be tempted and cheat. Maybe you feel assured that neither you nor your mate will be unfaithful, but you have an overall lack of trust that he or she has your best interest at heart. This creates a suspicion of your partner's motives and desires.

Many of you saw your parents did not have the family's best interest at heart as they decided to take care of their own needs and leave the family. If the two people you looked up to the most acted selfishly you learned that you could not trust them to do what was best for you or your family. If you consciously or unconsciously stopped trusting one or both of your parents as a result of the divorce you will most likely project the lack of trust you felt toward your parents on to your partner.

This was the case in our marriage. Neither of us felt we could trust our parents after their divorces. We did not trust them to have our best interest at heart. We did not trust the information our mothers gave us about our fathers, and we did not trust that our fathers would share accurate information about our mothers. This information was often skewed and negative and therefore hard to rely on. When we started dating, we never shared our relationship with our parents. Both of our mothers were so disillusioned about marriage that we just knew they would be negative. Also, we did not have faith in the guidance that they would give us. Many of us ACODPs do this because we don't feel we can trust our parents' relationship advice. We cannot trust their ability to see clearly what is healthy and what is not. Consequently, we ACODPs feel like we are navigating on the sea of marriage without a compass most of the time.

The Story of Us

From the very start of our relationship we had trouble trusting each other. Often we would project the lack of trust we felt about our parents on to each other. Because Tom's father had had repeated affairs, he came into our marriage with a great deal of suspicion. To make matters worse, I knew a great many people in college, including guys. When I would meet a guy on campus we might hug and chat for a while. I noticed that Tom would get very uncomfortable. He would make snide comments or say something slightly negative about the guy. One time I started to introduce him to one of my male friends and he walked away. He said that he had to talk to someone about an urgent matter. I thought it was strange so I questioned him about it. He became angry and highly reactive and started accusing me of being too flirtatious, too friendly with guys, and purposely trying to make him jealous. He said that he was not sure that he could trust me.

I was stunned. How could he accuse me of something so heinous? This crushed me. I tried to reason with him, but he was so upset that he walked away. His abandonment sent me into a panic and I became reactive. I followed him, clinging and crying, as I tried to convince him that I was trustworthy. But he had a hard time believing it. We were at such a loss. We were clearly overreacting in this situation, but we could not stop ourselves. We later learned that there was a reason for our extreme reactivity. We found out that we were reacting to the pain and trauma we experienced in our past and attaching it to our current relationship situation. This reactivity has a great deal to do with how traumatic memories are stored in the brain. To further explain this we need to give you brief lesson in neurobiology.

The Human Brain

The human brain is a marvelous machine capable of many advanced functions. It is divided into two basic parts—the cerebral cortex and the brain stem. The cerebral cortex is the highly advanced functioning part of humans. It is often referred to as the new brain. Humans are the only mammals that have a cerebral cortex or new brain. This is the part of the brain that enables humans to analyze information and make decisions. It also gives humans the ability to see themselves in their mind's eye and observe and critique their own behavior.

The brain stem, often referred to as the old brain, is the very primitive mammalian part of the human brain. It does not have the ability to take in information and observe human behavior. It can only react to the stimuli it receives. The limbic system is located at the root of the brain stem. It is the seat of very powerful emotions and is our self-defense monitor. It responds in a fight or flight manner when we are in real or perceived danger. There is something else that is very significant about the limbic system. It is atemporal, which means that it has no sense of time. Therefore, a memory that occurred at age five can be recalled at age twenty-five and bring up all of the sensations or emotions that a person felt at the time of the original trauma.

Neurobiologists have found that traumatic memories of childhood are stored in the old brain, not in the new brain. For many ACODPs the memories of their parents' divorces are traumatic. This was true for us. These traumatic memories are stored in the old brain. This can cause us a great deal of problems because as we recall the memories of our parents' divorces, we can not only feel the same hurt and pain that we experienced as children but these memories can also activate our self-defense mechanism, causing us to feel that we are in danger. If this happens, we usually respond in a fight or flight manner. Therefore, we are prone to have a situation that occurs in our marriage that triggers memories from childhood. We then feel many of the same painful emotions we felt as children. We overreact and have fight or flight responses when they may not be necessary. This causes a great deal of trouble in marriages.

Many people have difficulty believing in the power of the old brain. But just think for a moment about a time when you got really sick on a certain type of food. Perhaps you got a violent case of food poisoning.

Now think about that food. Do you feel a little nauseated as you recall this? That feeling of nausea is your old brain remembering the trauma you felt. We call this feeling an "old brainer."

I once got severe food poisoning and dehydration from eating salmon croquettes. I can't even say the term salmon croquettes without feeling sick to my stomach. This "yuck" response is my old brain self-defense mechanism serving as a reminder to me of past danger. The body does this to warn us of peril. Old brainers aren't so difficult to deal with when it comes to food triggers or upset stomachs, but what if these old brainers are triggered in the marriage? They can wreak havoc on it. This was the case with Tom and I. We had vivid memories of our parents' divorces. These memories would haunt us early in our marriage. If we would get in a conflict, many of these fight or flight responses were activated. We had no idea what was happening to us. So many of our responses were overreactive, but we seemed not to be able to control them. We later realized that our old brains were being triggered, and we were experiencing reactivity.

Reactivity

The definition of reactivity is using more emotion in a situation than it deserves. As we stated earlier, many painful memories of our past are stored in the old brain. These memories can be triggered and activated by stimuli in our present relationship. As these memories are triggered, we will overreact. This overreaction is called reactivity. We had many instances of reactivity early in our marriage. The following story illustrates a vivid example.

Our Story of Reactivity

When I was a young girl, I would listen to my parents fight, and I would become anxious and fearful because the conflicts would result in violence. Most of the time my father would leave and stay gone for days. He would not call or let us know where he was, so I would be sad and worried sick. As if this wasn't traumatic enough, I would be left with my angry, violent mother. Many times I feared for my own, and my siblings', safety. I would stay terrified for days and walk on eggshells trying to keep my mother peaceful and sane.

As the years went by I put these painful scenes in the back of my mind and tried to move on with my life. I thought that I was over them, but I did notice that I worried a lot, and I had a terrific fear of abandonment.

Some twenty years later as a bride of two months, I decided to cook dinner for my new husband. Since we were on a tight budget in graduate school, I found a very inexpensive recipe for quiche to prepare. I slaved hard in the kitchen to please my new groom, and was excited to show off my culinary skills. Unfortunately, there was a book that came out about that time called *Real Men Don't Eat Quiche.* I still want to meet the author and tell him just what I think of his work!

As I pridefully placed the perfect dish in front of Tom, he turned up his nose, and began telling me that real men did not eat such mushy egg dishes. This hurt my oversensitive feelings, so I whined and coerced, and he argued. This ridiculous debate was getting us nowhere. We were not making any headway in resolving our conflict, and our dinner was getting cold.

We continued to argue and Tom had finally had enough, so he stood up and announced, "I'm leaving. I'm gonna go out on the porch and cool off." When he was young his mother told him that all good, hot-blooded, Portuguese boys should cool off when they get mad. His mother taught him, in lieu of losing his temper, to go outside and calm down. One would think that I, his bride, would see the healthy rationale in this—but no! His leaving triggered the scenes from childhood where my father left and did not return. I had a major old brainer.

I panicked. I started to cry. "Please don't leave me," I whined and begged. He just looked at me like I was losing my mind. When he kept going I started accusing him of abandoning me. "How could you leave me? How could you be so mean and cold?" I cried. "What kind of man leaves a young bride who has slaved over a hot stove all afternoon?"

The danger bell rang in the limbic factory, and there I was: anxious, panicked, and full of fear. My trust in Tom, our relationship, and the entire institution of marriage was just about nonexistent at that time.

The more I clung, the more Tom wanted to escape. "What are you so upset about?" he asked incredulously. "Calm down. It's just dinner, for Pete's sake!" I continued to cry and he blew up and became reactive with me. My reactivity caused him to become reactive as well. Unbeknownst to me, I had triggered an old brain memory in Tom.

When his parents split, his mother confided in him, always telling him what a bad guy his father was. Tom became his mother's confidant, her surrogate husband. He hated her clinging to him and her enmeshment. It felt suffocating to him. When I was clinging to him, it triggered his old brain memories of his mother's enmeshment, and he overreacted to me and stormed out the door to try to get away.

It seemed that our marital conflict triggered memories from childhood, which activated my old brain, causing me to display reactivity. My reactivity toward Tom triggered his old brain memories and caused him to be reactive as well. In this scene, we see that my reactivity triggered Tom, and he became reactive, which further triggered me to become more reactive, which triggered him, and so it goes. This phenomenon is called interactivity, and it can create cycles in marriage which seem impossible to break.

At that point, we were not thinking like a young, sensible married couple. We were thinking like traumatized kids. I was thinking like an abandoned little girl, and Tom was thinking like an angry, enmeshed young man. My wounds interacted with his wounds and we were both reacting to each other with all of the emotions we felt as children. In soul-healing love theory we call this experience "interactivity."

Interactivity

Interactivity occurs when the soul wounds in one partner are triggered and he or she becomes reactive. His or her reactivity triggers the soul wounds in the other mate and now that mate is reactive as well. The soul wounds of one mate negatively interact with the soul wounds of the other mate, and thus interactivity occurs.

Interactivity is a very common phenomenon in marriage because individuals actually gravitate toward people with the same type of soul wounds. Often, this is an unconscious process. Even if you don't ask a person specifically what their childhood issues are, you may feel a sense of familiarity around them, that sense of, "I have known you all of my life." Later, as you get to know one another, you find that you have a lot in common, especially in your childhoods. This familiarity and comfort is what causes you to continue the relationship. If you are attracted to people who have wounds that are similar to your own, you will usually have opposite adaptations to some or all of those wounds. The person with a fear of abandonment wound will be attracted to the person with a fear of enmeshment wound. The loner will be attracted to the caretaker. The emotional "feeler" will be attracted to the unfeeling stoic.

When you first meet and start dating, you find that this opposite quality in your partner makes you feel complete and whole. As your relationship continues, these opposite adaptations cause many struggles. These same opposite adaptations to childhood wounds serve to hurt each other and push each other away. We say that these wounds are interactive, thus the term "interactivity."

You may think that the way to prevent this type of marital struggle is to marry someone who has the same type of wounds you do, so that interactivity will not occur. That way, you both will be clingers or both withdrawers. If this is the case then you won't trigger each other. Many of our clients say this, but we have found that people are usually not attracted to partners who are so similar. They are attracted to their opposite. This means that they will be attracted to someone who has opposite adaptations to their wounds as well.

Finding a new mate isn't the solution anyway. Divorce was our parents' way out, and many of them are no happier. The only way out is through. You must learn to deal with your reactivity and interactivity as it occurs. Old brainers can wreak havoc on ACODPs and their marriages, but they can be healed, if you are willing to learn how

False Conclusions

The quiche affair, as it was later called, taught us a great deal about how our old brainers were negatively affecting our marriage. In our reactivity, we drew false conclusions about each other, wrongly accusing each other of being like our parents. Nothing could be further from the truth. But at that moment, we were not in our right minds, or should we say, we were not in our new brains. We were in our old brains, so we could not see the situation clearly. We made up our own reality about each other.

As you can see, I had made up my own reality that Tom would leave me. I drew a false conclusion that he would do as my father had done in my past. This is where it gets tricky, because my indictment could have been so hurtful that he would actually have obliged me and left. In that case, I would have created a self-fulfilling prophecy.

Self-Fulfilling Prophecies

ACODPs create their own self-fulfilling prophecies all of the time. They can do this around many issues in marriage. But, it is never more destructive than when they do this in the area of trust. Earlier we learned that ACODPs have trouble with trust. This causes them to be easily triggered around trust issues. If they become suspicious, they might overreact and make false accusations about their partner. This causes their partner to react, and interactivity occurs. The accused partner may grow weary of defending him or herself. He or she figures that they are going to be accused anyway, so why keep trying to disprove a negative? The accused gives in to temptation and acts out his partner's worst fear. The unfortunate thing about this is that the accuser helped create the reality that he or she so greatly feared. The accuser actually shaped some of this self-fulfilling prophecy. This was the case with a couple we saw in our counseling center.

Melissa and Tim's Story

Melissa and Tim had been married only three years. They had a nine-month-old son, Timmy. Tim sold insurance and Melissa stayed home to raise Timmy. Melissa and Tim met at church. Tim's parents actually met Melissa first and introduced her to their son. His parents had been married for thirty-seven years. They were a very popular, likeable couple that taught Sunday school in their church. They were very fond of Melissa and she often referred to them as surrogate parents. She said that one of the biggest reasons she married Tim was his family. She admired her in-laws' commitment to marriage and family, and said that she wanted a mate with a stable heritage, because her parents divorced when she was twelve years old. Her mother had found out that her father had been having a long-term affair. Soon after that they divorced.

Both Melissa and Tim said their goal was to emulate Tim's parents' marriage. They were well on the road to doing this when Melissa started having trouble. This is when they came to us for counseling. It seems that Tim's job as an insurance salesman became increasingly troublesome for her. She grew tired of him working late and making home visits after dinner at night. With that tiredness, a suspicion grew. She began to question Tim about who he was with and how he was spending his time. She demanded he come home at 5:30 each day. When he said that was not possible she accused him of seeing another woman.

Tim was dumbfounded! He was an honest, trustworthy person, an eagle scout for Pete's sake! He would never cheat on Melissa. But by the time we saw them in therapy, he could not convince Melissa of his innocence. She was sure he was having an affair, and she could not trust him.

After a minimal amount of detective work it became evident that Tim was indeed trustworthy and that Melissa's suspicions were unfounded. It was our job to help this couple rebuild trust in their relationship. In order to do that we had to help Melissa understand that she was modeling the lack of trust which came from her parents' untrusting relationship, and she was projecting this lack of trust onto Tim.

Repeating patterns in our parents' marriages is a common phenomenon. We are all products of what we learn from our environment and Melissa had learned not to trust. Memories of her parents' mistrust, and the conflicts that ensued as a result, were etched into her old brain, and resurfaced when she had a conflict with Tim. When Tim would work late it would remind her of when her father came home late from work and her mother would be anxious and suspicious. Her parents would fight and the conflict would never get resolved. Melissa hated these tension-filled times. Tim's late hours triggered Melissa's fears and she would become suspicious and falsely accuse Tim of indiscretions.

When Melissa would accuse Tim, he would feel hurt and insulted. He could not understand her suspicions because he had grown up in a healthy, intact family that trusted each other and never questioned each other's fidelity or trustworthiness. This caused him a great deal of pain. As a result of the pain he would react by shutting down. This would thwart their communication and they could not resolve the conflict.

Melissa was reacting to an irrational process that made it hard for Tim to reason with her. He would ask rational questions such as "What have I done for you to stop trusting me?" Melissa could not answer because her irrational thoughts from childhood were consuming her and she was projecting them onto Tim. It helped her to learn that her old brain and reactivity could cause her to create falsehoods about her spouse, which can be hard to heal. They can cause her to make up realities about her partner that may not be accurate. The truth is what contradicts these falsehoods, and creates a new and positive image of her spouse. In Scripture, John 8:32 says, "Then you will know the truth, and the truth will set you free" (NIV). You see in Scripture that truth can provide freedom. Determining the truth about your partner can truly set you free.

Explaining old brainers and reactivity to Tim and Melissa actually relieved them and helped them understand why Melissa would get so irrational. We then helped her to find the truth in the situation. Melissa consciously knew that Tim was a very morally upright, caring husband who was not likely to cheat. But when she was triggered, she threw all that out the window and stopped trusting him. Two things helped her get out of this dilemma and see reality. One was her awareness that she was having old brainers around the issue of trust and that these issues were tied to her past and not to her relationship with Tim. The other was becoming aware of the truth and believing it. To help Melissa see the truth we had her do an exercise that we designed called the True Vision Exercise.

THE TRUE VISION EXERCISE

This exercise is designed to help individuals who have a particularly bad or negative image of their partner as a result of their childhood wounds. It enables the ACODP begin to see the truth about his or her mate. This technique allows a person to get a vision of who his or her spouse actually is, and it also helps neutralize the reactivity which comes from the soul wounds of the past. Completing this exercise can alleviate the tendency for a person to put the unhealthy faces of their caretakers onto their spouse. Melissa learned to get a true clear vision of Tim after doing this exercise.

Here is how it works. Draw a line down the center of a piece of paper, making two columns. At the top of the right column write the word "Beliefs." Under this column write all of the false beliefs that have been a part of your thinking as a result of your soul wounds. At the top of the left column write the word "Evidence." Now, move into the logical, rational, left side of the brain. This is the side that makes decisions on facts not feelings. Under this column write all the objective observable realities that you know to be true. List all the data you can to prove that your impression or idea is true. You may use what your partner says and does, as well as background information, as means of determining the truth as objectively as possible. Following is an example of how Melissa did this exercise.

Under the Beliefs column Melissa wrote:

- My father cheated on my mother, therefore men are not to be trusted.
- Most men cheat.
- My husband will cheat.
- Since my mother wasn't enough to keep my father, then I will not be enough to keep Tim.

Then Melissa was to list the Evidence showing whether Tim was like her father and other men she knew. Melissa was to make a list of all of the ways Tim was trustworthy that she knows to be true. Here is a sample from Melissa's list:

- Tim is a good, moral man.
- He goes to church almost every Sunday and believes in the Ten Commandments.
- He was raised to know that cheating is wrong.
- He has a great example of fidelity in his parents.
- He loves the baby and me.
- He never flirts or acts interested in other women.
- He tells me regularly that he "only has eyes for me."

We instructed Melissa to make several copies of this list and put it where she would see it several times a day—on the bathroom mirror, on the fridge, in the kitchen, or taped on the computer monitor. Melissa was then to read the list every time she walked by a copy and repeat it to herself. Whenever she felt triggered by Tim coming home late or having a female client, she would read the list again. Eventually this repetition began to reprogram her old brain and her reactivity subsided. Researchers have found that replication, that is repeating a process over and over, is the best way to reprogram trauma from childhood. This worked for Melissa. She then learned to trust in Tim and the fact that their marriage would not end like her parents' did. Knowing and believing the truth truly set this couple free.

In order to overcome this inability to trust, many of us are going to have to become aware of the issues in our lives that taught us not to trust. Many of these issues centered around our parents' divorces.

Then, we will have to use an exercise like the True Vision Exercise to reprogram our thinking with the truth. This truth will free us and help heal our trust wounds as ACODPs.

Chapter 5

The Fear Wound

Years ago there was a Nike shoe commercial about an athlete who rose to some great sporting challenge. I don't remember the athlete or the particular sport. But I do remember the slogan. In bold letters across the screen it read, No Fear. This statement stuck in my mind. I think the reason that it impacted me so much was because I had so much fear. In fact I couldn't imagine my life without it. This fear has been with me as far back as I can remember. I think it comes with the territory of being an adult child of divorced parents. There is the fear of being abandoned, which plagued me, the fear of failure, which became Tom's nemesis, the fear that love will stop, the fear of doom, that things will go wrong, and many others.

We are aware that these fears can come from other types of dysfunctional families. I inherited a great deal of fear from living in violence and abuse. But the fears we are referring to appear to be indigenous to ACODPs. Many adult children of divorce tell us that these fears afflict their marriage. One of the most common is the fear of doom.

The Fear of Doom

This fear can take on many forms. ACODPs may fear that their marriage will not last. They fear that bad things will happen to them. They live in constant fear that what happened to their parents will happen to them. They worry that their partner will come home one day and announce that they are no longer in love or that they want a divorce. They have a haunting fear that their marriage will end. Some are not consciously aware that this fear is troubling them; they just know that they feel a vague sense of doom most of the time.

Several years ago a couple came into our counseling center. They had been married about two years. They were in their late thirties and had waited until they were older to marry because they really wanted to be sure that they knew what they wanted in a mate. They also wanted to prevent making a mistake in choosing a lifelong partner. Both of them were adult children of divorced parents, and both of them said that their parents' divorces were very traumatic for them.

The interesting thing about this couple is that they started by telling us that their marriage was really good. They had made sure that they were compatible long before they decided to marry each other. They communicated well, and both had a genuine love and even friendship with each other. They fought infrequently, but constructively, and they had a great deal of fun together. So we wondered why they felt they needed marital counseling. It seems that they both had a constant fear that something was going to go wrong at any time. They both felt a sense of doom, that the curtain was going to fall, and that things would fall apart.

As they shared their childhood stories, we learned that they both described their parents' marriages as good and their childhoods as normal and happy. Neither of them had a clue that their parents were in trouble. Both of them said that the announcement of the breakup of their respective families came as a complete shock to them. They both shared this feeling of disbelief and betrayal. We explained to them that this fatal surprise was inexplicable to them. They could not make sense of what was happening to their families. They were shocked and traumatized by something they never saw coming. This created a deep fear in them that things would not work out in the end. This manifested as a cloud of doom that hovered over their marital bliss and caused them to worry that something bad would happen when they least expected it.

We realized that what this couple needed most from us was assurance. They needed to know that they were doing things right, which would help them avert the disaster of divorce. We shared with them how ACODPs manifest many fears, and that their fear of impending doom is normal, considering their circumstances. They were actually relieved to hear that their fears were common. This calmed them down enough to see all the good that they had developed in their marriage and eased their fears tremendously. They were grateful that we normalized their struggles. This gave them the strength and motivation to face these fears, and challenge them with the truth. After a few brief sessions, they continued on their marital journey, minus the doomsday cloud.

Tom and I both brought the fear of doom into our marriage. This fear was pervasive in our relationship and manifested itself in many specific ways. I carried with me a constant feeling that the other shoe would drop. Tom feared disaster would befall us when we least expected it. These fears created some very difficult patterns for us. We would like to tell you about a few of them.

Fear of Abandonment

There is a particular type of abandonment wound that seems to trouble adult children of divorced parents. In Chapter 1, you read a study in which the majority of the female participants perceived their parents' divorces and the subsequent loss of their fathers as rejection. These girls felt that they were not pretty enough, smart enough, or talented enough to get their fathers to pay attention to them or visit more frequently. I could have been a participant in that study. This is exactly how I perceived my father's leaving.

Because of the strong rejection I felt after my parents' divorce, I became a super performer. I made the honor roll, I was a leader in my church youth group, and I became drum majorette and led the band. Subconsciously, I did all of this to win my parents' approval. I wanted my mom to be happy again, and I wanted my dad to visit more. When my performance did not work, I tried harder, repeating an endless cycle of tasks and never getting the reward I was looking for.

Consequently, I took this performance mentality and oversensitivity into our marriage. I think that from the time that I met Tom and fell in love with him, I started to fear that he would leave me. This fear played out in many ways. It caused me to be too clingy, the constant pursuer, who would whine for his affection. If he would say he was going to the grocery store to get milk, I wanted to tag along. I did not like to be away from him, so I did not give him a lot of space. I always felt that he never paid enough attention to me and I would drone on and on about it. This left Tom feeling overwhelmed and suffocated. He felt like he could never do enough to meet my needs. Eventually, he stopped trying so hard and started playing the role of distancer to escape my enmeshment. I continued to play the role of pursuer to try to quell my fear. Our early games of Marital Pac Man were very frustrating for both of us.

The fear of abandonment also caused me to want to be useful so that I would not be deserted. I felt that if I was needed, then I would not be left behind. In order to ensure my importance, I became a caretaker. After my parents' divorce, my mother went to work and I became my family's caretaker. I would care for my mother, my siblings, and my dad when he visited us.

I especially wanted my dad's visits to be perfect so he would come more often. During these times, I would be the perfect child, always making sure that the siblings were well behaved, that the circumstances were pleasant, and that he was all right. This meant that I had to be bossy and maternal to my siblings a lot of the time. They did not want to take orders from me because I was just an older sister and not an authority figure so they would rebel against me causing even more problems. In my frustration to make things good for everyone, I ignored how I felt and put my dad's needs above my own. I would like to say that my motives were noble, and that this was a healthy, loving response, but my codependency was very unhealthy and my motives were selfish. My caretaking was to get my father's love and approval.

Meanwhile at home, I played the caretaker role as well. I would calm my mother when she would have a volatile episode. As she ranted and raved, I would try to pacify her and get my siblings out of harm's way. I cooked and cleaned and cared for my younger siblings. I was the pervasive peacemaker, the perennial placater, and the consummate caretaker. All of these were altruistic, but unfortunately, very sick!

Caretaking is not an altogether bad thing. But the problem with me being this kind of caretaker is that my actions were motivated by fear. Because of this fear, I could never let my real feelings surface. I was not authentic. I played a role. I was a phony, and I didn't even know it. I was afraid to let the real me come out. The few times I was honest with my mother and let my frustrations come out, she beat me and told me that I was being disrespectful. I learned from this to hide my real self deep down within my soul, and be what everyone wanted me to be. I had internalized this fear of abandonment into a basic message that became a theme for me. The internal message read, "If I am the real me, you won't like me." I carried this role into my marriage because of my profound fear that Tom would abandon me as well. Little did I know that because of the role I played, I was actually creating a reason for him to leave.

The paradox was that I was kind and caring so that Tom would not leave, but in being this way, my lack of honesty about my true feelings made him want to leave. Tom could not relate to me. When we would share, instead of telling him what I really felt, I would tell him what I thought he wanted to hear. I would respond with some placating and caring reply, but it was not genuine or real. One would think that he would be thrilled to have such a "perfect" wife. The irony was that he would have rather had a real wife than a "perfect" one any day. I was just too afraid of rejection to let my true self come out. The more I appeased, the more frustrated he became. He found my caretaking tedious and fake. I found it unreal and unrewarding, but my fear wouldn't let me get out of this role and behavior pattern.

In Tom's frustration and anger, he would try to get me to respond genuinely. He would even try to provoke me, to get me to be more truthful about feelings. He would say things such as, "You make me so mad. I'm not going to talk to you if you won't be honest." I would respond much like the cerebral Dr. Spock in the *Star Trek* television series. I would say something such as, "What makes you feel this way?" My stoic, holier-than-thou demeanor would infuriate him. The angrier he became, the more cerebral I became. He called this process "therapizing" and said that he hated when I "therapized" him. He said it made him feel like a client, not a partner. In his frustration, he would then make deadly comments such as, "This isn't working, so I might as well just leave." We later realized that these comments were rooted in his fear of failure, but they would grossly trigger my abandonment wound even more.

We call these types of trigger statements "impact statements" because they impact one's soul wounds in such a negative way. As these impact statements hit my soul wounds, I would react by becoming even more clinging and pursuing. I would even further caretake the situation. This would set Tom off, and interactivity between us would occur. We were in a vicious game of Marital Pac Man and we could not get out of it.

In order for me to be real with my feelings, I had to get in touch with the fear that was causing my behavior. Then I had to challenge this fear and overcome it. We will share more about how to do this later in this chapter, but first, we want to tell you about another fear that plagues ACODPs.

Fear of Failure: Tom's Story

While Bev struggled with fear of abandonment, I was struggling with a fear of my own. I had a tremendous fear of failure. As a kid, I felt like it was my job to keep my parents together, and I always feared that I would fail. When their marriage finally did end, I felt like I had let everyone in my family down, including myself.

I was very intuitive and aware of the dynamics between my parents. Early on, I began to take responsibility for the outcome of their relationship. I especially took responsibility for my mother and her feelings. Like Bev, I played the role of my mother's caretaker. Unlike her however, I did not take to this position very well. I hated sublimating my feelings to make sure that my mother was all right. I detested watching what I said or did so that I would not incur her displeasure. I did not like it when Mom would whine and complain about my dad. I grew impatient when she would want to cling to me and confide in me. Needless to say, I did not play the role favorably. I can't blame her; she needed someone to talk to, but I did not think it should be her son. This phenomenon of parents clinging to their children to get their own emotional needs met is referred to as emotional incest.

Dr. Patricia Love in her book, *The Emotional Incest Syndrome: When a Parent's Love Rules Your Life*, defines emotional incest as the unhealthy bond between a parent and a child, in which the child's needs are disregarded in order to meet the parent's needs. The parent may even elevate the child to a special place in his or her life. Dr. Love calls the child the chosen child. Trust me, there is nothing special or chosen about this position. I had to be my mom's surrogate husband. This role suffocated me and caused me to incur my father's wrath.

It became obvious after a while that Mom liked me better than she liked Dad. She would praise me for being there for her. She would say things like, "You are always there for me. You will always listen." Underneath the compliment, I heard the subliminal, implied message, "Don't have any feelings or needs of your own. Meet my needs instead." This sense of responsibility was overwhelming to me. The enmeshment strangled me. I would tolerate it as long as I could, then I would snap at her in anger. Mom would cry. I would feel guilty and pull away in anger and frustration. Once again, I would resume the role of her caretaker. This caused me to resent closeness, and fear being swallowed in close relationships.

Like Bev, I too had internalized messages that became themes for my life. In this case, I developed an inner belief that, "If I get close to you, I will lose me." This caused me to distance myself from intimate relationships. I became a loner, an island, not needing anyone. I felt better off by myself, because then I would not fear being swallowed or sublimating my feelings, needs, and desires.

If I couldn't make my mother happy, or I couldn't fix my parents' marital problems, then I would feel like a failure. My parents' intense marital struggles lasted from the time I was thirteen until I was twenty-five years old. They were in and out of the marriage, breaking up, then getting back together several times. During that time, I played the role of the healer. Internally, I knew that I was in a no-win situation. But I was stuck there. I resented it, fearing failure at every turn. When their marriage eventually failed, I felt that in some way, I had failed too. I internalized an inner belief about failure as well. I believed that, "No matter how hard you try, things will not work out in the end."

Because my parents' marriage had failed, I felt terribly responsible for making my marriage work. This meant in my mind that I had to do everything to make Bev happy. Because I was sensitive, I would read a look on her face or an innocent gesture as meaning in some way that she was not happy, and that it was my fault. Many times, that fear of failure would cause me to feel very guilty because I could not fix everything. Like most males, I typically expressed fear and guilt by getting angry. I would explode at Bev for triggering these negative feelings. She would cry in response to my harshness, which would activate more guilt and fear of failure and so goes the cycle of our interactivity. This cycle sent us both cascading into despair and hopelessness.

We now know that the more a person internalizes a fear, the more they will generalize it, thus they will be inclined to maximize it. This means that a person's internalized fear will come out in many general areas of their life and that often they will maximize that fear, especially in intimate relationships.

Internalize, Generalize, Maximize

This is what we did in our marriage. We internalized our fears. We carried them deep within us and felt their ever-present essence in our souls. They became a part of us. They defined us, and our relationship with each other. It wasn't long before our internalized fears became generalized to other areas of life. These generalized fears became the themes of our lives. Bev's generalized theme was, "I must be perfect for you to love me." Tom's generalized theme was, "No matter what I do, I won't be loved." We both maximized these themes in our relationship. Bev would placate and try to please, clinging and whining all the way. Tom would fear failure, and distance and withdraw. Before we knew it we were deep into the cycle of interactivity. In the early years of our marriage, it would take us days to recover from our own reactive fear. Ultimately, we had to come to the point of learning how to take responsibility for our fear, rather than reacting to it.

We learned that we had nothing to fear but fear itself. Our marriage was not destined to fail simply because our parents' marriages had failed. We began to realize that we could consciously do things to heal our marriage, no matter what our fear told us. One of the ways that we consciously healed our relationship was to replace fear and reactivity with intentionality.

Intentionality

The definition of intentionality is the ability to act in a healthy manner, no matter how you feel. It is a notion that is used in self-help groups involving addictive behaviors like alcoholism or drug addiction. "Fake it till you make it" is the more idiomatic term for this concept. In other words, act in a healthy fashion, no matter what you are feeling.

Alcoholics Anonymous teaches that even if you are desperate for a drink, walk past the bar door and act as if you do not want one. Even when you are dying for a drink, withstand it any way. After a while, your feelings will follow your behavior. Many AA participants refer to this as "white knuckle sobriety." This means staying sober by an act of your will, not your feelings or emotions. In our marriage we developed what we call "white knuckle matrimony." We consciously proposed to act in a healing manner, no matter how afraid we were. One wonderful thing about intentionality is that you can't practice it and be reactive. Intentionality and fear do not mix. If you pick one, you can't have the other.

At times this was very hard, especially when certain fears would rear their ugly heads to remind us of the past. Still, we kept trudging. Not because we were so strong or courageous, quite the contrary. We just knew that we wanted our marriage to work. Years ago, as we were dealing with our fears, we heard a saying that, "Courage is just fear that has said its prayers." We learned that when we changed our behavior and acted with intentionality no matter how we actually felt at the time, positive emotions eventually followed. We encourage you as ACODPs, if fear is worrying your marriage, to practice intentionality.

Dealing with your fear is facing it directly. In order to do this you will need to ask yourself some questions. We have developed an exercise designed to help you answer some important questions in an organized fashion, so you can see how fear has affected you as an ACODP. We call this exercise the IGMP (pronounced "I gump"). The acronym makes the steps easier to remember as you try to defeat your fear. The steps to dealing with and overcoming your fear are:

Internalize: the fearful messages I send myself
Generalize: how I feel this fear in the general areas of my life
Maximize: how I overreact to this fear in my intimate relationships
Pulverize: the way in which I challenge my fear and defeat it

The IGMP Exercise lists these steps and asks several questions in each category to help you become aware of your fears as an ACODP. Following is an example of Tom's IGMP to show you how it works.

Tom's IGMP Exercise

Internalize:
- **What are you afraid of in your life and marriage?**
  I am afraid of failing in my life and in my marriage. I am afraid that Bev will stop loving me.
- **What is your internal message about that fear?**
  My internal message is that I am not lovable and that I will fail, no matter how hard I try.
- **Where did you learn this?**
  I learned this by watching my parents strive and struggle and still not be able to make their marriage work. I also felt that I failed, too, because I could not keep them together. My mom was clingy and needy and I felt like I could not meet her emotional needs. My Dad was critical and I felt like I never measured up to his expectations. All of this contributed to my fear of failure.

Generalize:
- **Do you believe this internalization applies to other areas of your life?**
  Yes, I am hard on myself in many areas of my life.
- **What are those areas?**
  I struggle with inadequacy issues as a husband and a father, and I hate to mess up. I take it hard if I feel like I have let my family down. I also set high expectations for myself vocationally, in writing and speaking, and judge myself too harshly sometimes.

Maximize:
- **What are the life themes that you have developed from these generalizations?**
  I fear that no matter how hard I try, nothing will work out in the end.
  I fear that I am not good enough or lovable enough.

- **How do you maximize these generalizations in your marriage?**
  When I feel like I can't make Bev or the kids happy, I feel guilty. This makes me mad, so I respond in anger. My anger causes them and me to distance and I feel hopeless and even more like a failure.

Pulverize:

- **As a result of my answers in this exercise, what patterns would I like to change?**
  I want to feel successful. I want to quit taking responsibility for others' happiness. I want to quit feeling guilty and that I am not good enough.
- **Challenge your life themes in light of the truth. List those challenges.**
  My parents' divorce was not my fault.
  I am not a failure, just because their marriage failed.
  My marriage will not fail.
  I have faith to combat fear.
  I am successful.
  I am good enough.
  I am lovable because God loves me just the way I am.

Speaking these truths disputes the lies that we have been taught all of our life. Telling ourselves these truths renews us. It gives us faith to combat our fears as ACODPs. Romans 12:2b says, "Be ye transformed by the renewing of your mind (NIV)." Impressing these correct and honest messages on our minds daily brings healing for our fear. Now take some time and do your own IGMP Exercise.

EXERCISE: THE IGMP EXERCISE: INTERNALIZE, GENERALIZE, MAXIMIZE, AND PULVERIZE

Answer the following questions and share the answers with your spouse.

Internalize:

- **What are you afraid of in your life and marriage?**
- **What is your internal message about that fear?**

- **Where did you learn this?**

Generalize:
- **Do you believe this internalization applies to other areas of your life?**
- **What are those areas?**

Maximize:
- **What are the life themes that you have developed from these generalizations?**
- **How do you maximize these generalizations in your marriage?**

Pulverize:
- **As a result of my answers in this exercise, what patterns would I like to change?**
- **Challenge your life themes in light of the truth. List those challenges.**

Fears Are Irrational

Most fears are irrational. Challenging the unfounded negative messages that cause these fears will help you see that you do not have to be afraid. This exercise enables you to do this. It helped Bev and I to dispute our worries, and learn the truth about our marriage and about ourselves. It took a great deal of time and patience for me to feel successful. It was equally hard for Bev to be real and honest about her feelings. She struggled with feeling vulnerable and exposed. I wrestled with being more of a pursuer than a distancer. We consciously tried to encourage each other to abolish the fears that haunted us. We worked hard on reprogramming our old brainers with new messages of love and support. It was hard work, and we faltered at times, but eventually we became each other's greatest cheerleaders for team ACODP. We knew that we were in this game of marriage together and that we were going to win. You can win too, if you face your fears.

Chapter 6

The Insecurity Wound

Webster defines insecurity as the lack of confidence, not safe, exposed, or liable to risk and danger, not firmly or reliably placed or fastened. We saw in the first chapter that ACODPs inherit a great many problems. They have higher rates of depression, anxiety, and chemical dependency. To add to this, they have lower rates of self-esteem and diminished learning capacity. Suffice it to say that these troubles can create a great deal of insecurity in us. In life we can feel unsafe, exposed, at risk, or in danger. The feeling that we have not been firmly or reliably placed in this world haunts us as ACODPs. This often makes us feel that we have to work harder than adult children of intact families just to survive.

Bev's Story

When I think of the word insecurity, I tend to think of the term shaky. That fits for me. I have felt shaky most of my life. It is as if something inside of me would not stay still. I spent most of my life with the trembling feeling of lingering insecurity. I felt insecure as a woman. I felt insecure as a prospective partner on the dating and mating scene. I felt insecure as a wife to Tom, and I felt insecure as a professional. In working with countless ACODPs over the last twenty-two years, I have learned that these insecurities are common. They have many manifestations. ACODPs can manifest insecurity by not feeling confident in intimate relationships, and not adapting to change well. One very widespread adaptation to these insecurities is the need for control.

Control Issues

Many ACODPs feel that their childhood was chaotic. Things happened in their parents' marriages that they could not manage or control. This feeling of being out of control created a sense of insecurity and hopelessness. They internalized a message that they must be in control at all times to avert possible disaster. Tom and I both felt this way.

We both took too much responsibility for our parents' divorces, so we both were plagued with a sense of despair when they finally split. To combat this, we became controlling. Having two control freaks in marriage is deadly! As we have learned in previous chapters, Tom and I have very similar childhood wounds, but opposite adaptations to these wounds. Our insecurity wounds and control issues were no exception.

I adapted to the insecurity in my family by being the overachiever, the overdoer, and the extremely driven one. I loved control, I loved having my way, and I was sure that I was right most of the time. If this sounds sanctimonious, that's because it is. Tom, on the other hand, adapted to his insecurity wounds with a more subtle need to control. His was more covert. He often used passive-aggressive anger to make his point.

There was one particular scene early in our marriage that illustrates this. When we first got married we were in graduate school and did not have a lot of money. I was a real "penny pincher." I learned to be tight with money in response to my father's leaving and our family's income dropping drastically. After he left we had very little money to make ends meet. The upside of this situation was that I learned how to stretch a dollar; the downside was that it left me with deep insecurities and worries about money.

Tom grew up in a middle-class family, so he did not worry about money as much as I did. He was grown when his parents divorced so he did not feel as much financial pressure after his father left. Because of my worry over money, I controlled the checkbook. I hovered over it like a mother hen guards her prize eggs. This drove Tom crazy. I wanted him to account for every penny. I gave him an allowance, and made him a sack lunch everyday, to save money. Any time he tried to ask me to loosen up on the purse strings, I had a solid reason for him to save his pennies. Often, when we would argue, he would say, "I just can't win with you. You are always right." My smug response was, "Then prove me wrong." He couldn't, so I got my way. I won the control battle and lost the love war. The writer of the Book of Proverbs says, "You must eat the bitter fruit of having your own way" (1:31 TLB). My control victories may have eased my insecurities, but they were not sweet.

One day, we were eating breakfast in our honeymoon haven and Tom broke his juice glass. "Oh, well," I replied, "We will just have to wait till the jelly is gone to get another glass." Our juice glasses were a fine collection of cheap jelly and jam jars. Tom protested, "Surely we have enough money to buy juice glasses." "That's frivolous!" I retorted. We then got into an argument about whether we should have juice glasses. Of course, I tried to control and took the thrifty high road, stating that we needed to be good stewards of our money and not spend it on unnecessary things. This really bothered Tom. He tried to tell me how he felt, but he knew that I would ultimately control the situation. So, instead of getting into a losing battle with me, he became passive-aggressive.

The definition of passive-aggressive behavior is acting out your aggression in a passive, covert way. Rather than being overt or assertive, the passive-aggressive person acts surreptitiously. They feel that in order to get their way they must do things secretively. That day when I came home from work, I looked in the cupboard and there sat six shiny new juice glasses. And, he had purchased them with a credit card. We had to pay interest on those frivolous objects. Now that is passive-aggressive anger at its best. There is a saying that passive-aggressive people don't get mad, they get even. Tom sure evened the score that day.

I wish that I could say that after that extremely unhealthy episode, we came to our senses, talked out our difficulties, and relinquished control. But that was not the case. Unfortunately, we spent several struggling years trying to resolve our control issues before we made any headway. In dealing with them we had to look at our behavior and see what it was doing to our marriage.

A Look in the Mirror

The first place we wanted to look was at each other. We could have given you a long list of offenses that our partner was doing that were unhealthy and destructive. We each were certain that our problems were with each other, not within ourselves. When we tried to talk, we both just pointed at the speck in each other's eye and did not look at the log in our own. This was getting us nowhere.

Years later, as we were completing our certification in Imago Relationship Therapy, one of our homework assignments was to write a brief essay about what we were like to live with. We had to ask ourselves this very important question, "What is it like living with me?" Being the spiritual people we are, we felt that we needed to take this assignment seriously and do a personal inventory of ourselves. This made us look in the mirror and examine our motives, wants, and desires in our relationship. Rather than blaming each other and pleading our cases, we took a look at ourselves.

At that time in our marriage, I could have given you a list of the negative things about living with Tom, but I hadn't really thought about what it was like to live with me. This was probably because I was thinking that most of the problems were Tom's fault, and that I was right the majority of the time.

In order to answer the question properly, we gave each other permission to interview people we lived with growing up to see what insights they could give us. I piously ran off to do my assignment with my interviewees in mind. First, I called my twin sister. She was my roommate for eighteen years, and one of my closest friends; surely she would be a good judge of what a wonderful person I was. Her testimony would surely shine the light on my angelic qualities and thus point to the devilish Tom as the real culprit in our struggles.

I phoned her, and told her that I was doing a project on what it was like living with me and that I would like her to give me some information. "Why, living with you was great," she eagerly volunteered. "You were generous, compassionate, caring, a good listener, and a great friend." "Hey, this is going great," I thought pridefully. "This will really make my case." As my sister continued, I really started feeling puffed up. "You are deeply spiritual, kind hearted and hard working. Now, do I get to tell you about how controlling you were?"

"Well," I harrumphed, "I think I need to go now," I said, as I ended the call in a bit of a huff. The mere idea that she would say such a thing. My case against Tom was diminishing right before my eyes.

I knew what I had to do then. I had to find another supporter to help build my argument. I would interview my younger brother. He would support my defense; after all, I practically raised him. He would be my ally. I called him and asked the key question, "What is it like living with me?" "Oh," he said, "you were generous and kind." "Good, good," I thought to myself. "This is working." "Continue," I said encouragingly.

"You were always very thoughtful, and I could wake you up at 2 A.M. to cook me grits and gravy and you would do it." "This is going nicely," I pridefully pondered. He continued, "When do I get to comment about how bossy you were?"

Well that was it! "Thank you very much," I stated in the most martyrish tone I could muster. "I'll have to talk to you later." I was truly beside myself. These evaluations were biased and skewed. "That's it," I thought to myself. "They are bogus. They must be. I'm a wonderful person with wonderful motives. I only bossed and controlled because they needed it. They were better off because of it, right?"

Boy, was I deluded. I thought that because my motives were benevolent and that I was trying to take care of everybody and everything, that my controlling behavior was okay. But it wasn't. The people in my environment did see the good that I was trying to do, but they also struggled with the unhealthy way in which I did it. I had to come face to face with my flaws. I had to look in the mirror and see my faults. This was so painful for me. I now know why.

Perfect Person Syndrome

I now realize that I was I was afflicted with a disease that is deadly for relationships. Since then, we have actually named this affliction. We call this lethal relationship virus The Perfect Person Syndrome. It afflicts many do-gooder control freaks like myself. ACODPs tend to fall prey to this problem for several reasons. One is because they fear change. The change that occurred in their families-of-origin caused them great pain. The other reason is that the insecurity they feel in intimate relationships makes them have high expectations and desire perfection. These afflicted persons have very good motives. They want everyone to be happy and all things to go well. That is why they control. They do not try to abuse their power or dominate others; they just want to avert disaster. They feel that in order to do this successfully, they must be in control at all times. So you see, their control is benevolent. They do not want to hurt other people; they just want to help.

So how could this be bad? It is bad because no one person should be in control of the marriage. It is unhealthy because it does not allow for control and power to be shared in the relationship, not to mention that it puts too much pressure on the control freak. I had this malady, and because of it, I thought that I was right most of the time. My points were lucid, logical, and often Biblical and I could win a debate. I unconsciously thought, "Just do it my way and everything will be okay." However, there is a huge problem with The Perfect Person Syndrome. Even if you are well intended, you leave no room for your partner to have his or her opinions. This causes them to feel dismissed, unimportant, and just plain bad. This is what I was doing to Tom and I did not even see it.

To finish our assignment in the Imago training, we had to report our findings to each other and discuss what we discovered from our friends and relatives about what it was like living with us. As I started to share my findings with Tom, I knew that I needed to be truthful, but my pride was getting in the way. I willingly and eagerly shared all the positives. "I'm generous, compassionate, a good friend, a good helper, kind-hearted, and caring." I really wanted to stop in that complimentary state. That sounded so nice, but I knew that I needed to confess *all* of my findings. So in a mumbled low tone, much like a used car salesman who practically whispers the price of a car as he shares all its attributes, I managed to quickly and quietly quip, "Oh, and by the way, I'm a little bossy and controlling."

"What?" Tom questioned, with a gleam in his eye. "I didn't hear those last two. Could you say them again, a little slower and a little louder?" I had been caught and I knew it. I had to eat crow and I didn't like it. I managed to muster the courage that humility requires and grunted, "My siblings say that I am bossy and a little controlling." At that moment, the moment of confession, I saw myself. For the first time in our marriage, I did not defend my good intentions. I did not protect my noble motives. I just confessed the truth. In doing this, I saw what it was really like living with me.

Oh, I was generous and all the rest, *but*, and this was a big *but*, I was indeed bossy and controlling. For years, Tom had tried to tell me that I was hard to live with because of this. But I would justify and rationalize my position. My Perfect Person Syndrome just would not let me see my mistakes. For the first time, I saw them glaring back at me, and I was truly humbled. This humility was the beginning of my growth.

Tom's Insight

It is an interesting phenomenon, in terms of how we are attracted to one another, that we have very similar wounds and opposite adaptations. Both Bev and I were wounded in the area of insecurity in relationships, and similarly, we both learned to caretake our family systems. The difference in our adaptations to these wounds was that Bev became the consummate caretaker, while I cared for my family just enough to suffice, and then I withdrew. Often, my withdrawal would be secretive and covert. I would slip off to my room and hide away, without anyone in my family knowing. I did this to protect myself, but it developed a very passive-aggressive behavior pattern for me. I would typically try to do whatever I could so that Bev would be happy in the relationship, observing her reactions to my efforts to please her. If I sensed at any point that she was still unhappy, rather than giving more to the relationship, I would withdraw and become passive-aggressive.

I would resent her control and criticism, which unconsciously reminded me of my mother's enmeshment and my father's disparagement. Feeling controlled by Bev made me feel inadequate and insecure, much like it did in my childhood. The more I felt insecure, the more I became passive-aggressive. Since I perceived her control as criticism of me, I found myself thinking about and doing things to prove that I was adequate. Unfortunately, these things were very irrational, like buying juice glasses on credit to prove that we needed them. She would try to control my spending regarding even the smallest things, which made me want to buy those things all the more. When I would try to make my case, Bev was a better debater than I was. After all, her motives were so "noble," and I found myself unable to talk about how I really felt. It was so frustrating to have an encounter with Bev about spending money that I was tempted to actually do things that would upset her, much like a rebellious adolescent who reacts to overcontrolling, critical parents.

Asking myself the question, "What is it like living with me?" was hard because I wanted to put most of the blame for our relationship struggles onto Bev. I realized that my passive-aggressive behavior was really an adaptation to my own insecurity. While she exacerbated it with her control, I had to take responsibility for my unhealthy behavior. The more I acted out in our relationship, the more I was proving that I really was inadequate and insecure. My own passive-aggressive behavior was actually reinforcing my insecurity, and enabling Bev's control. In essence, the very thing that I was doing, in reacting to my wounds, was unconsciously reinforcing them.

After one of these encounters I usually felt even more lonely and depressed. I realized that I had become moody, sullen, and withdrawn, just like my father. In spite of my best conscious efforts, I had become the very thing I feared most. I saw that I was not consciously doing this, but that I was simply reacting to my own woundedness, and I also realized that my behavior and withdrawal was impacting Bev's insecurity as well. We both began to understand that something had to change in this dance of interactivity that we were doing.

It was very humbling and even embarrassing to have to admit my passive-aggressive behavior to Bev. I told her that I was angry and that I was acting out that anger in very unhealthy ways. Looking in the mirror, instead of at Bev to find the fault in our marriage, I saw that I was projecting my own insecurity onto her. Instead of owning my behavior, I justified it, telling myself that Bev was just controlling and fearful. I perceived her as the insecure one and believed that my response was the only "logical" remedy. Projecting my own insecurity onto her kept me from having to face it in myself. Answering the question, "What is it like living with me?" caused us to get our eyes off of each other and onto ourselves, where the real healing needed to take place. We realized that we projected so much negative behavior onto each other in order to keep from looking at our own woundedness.

Projection

Projection is creating a perception that your partner is the one with the issue, not you. It is the act of visualizing an idea in your mind as an objective reality. We learned earlier that we tend to make up realities about our partner. In relationships, we see things through our own clouded perspective, which may not be completely accurate. Projection is a way in which we cloud our perspective and attribute the feelings, thoughts, and attitudes that are present within us onto another person. By doing this, we do not have to own or deal with these characteristics within ourselves.

We once worked with a client who spent exorbitant amounts of money on lavish trips for he and his wife. They came into therapy because they could not resolve their conflicts over money. She was really upset about their poor financial state. He said that he planned these trips because his wife wanted to go and he really wanted to give her what she wanted. As the therapy progressed, his wife confided that she did not really like to travel. She would rather save money and get their finances in order. He was terribly upset and kept insisting that she was the one who wanted these expensive vacations. It took him a while to realize that he was projecting his desire for escape and adventure onto his wife. He felt that it was selfish to say that he was doing it for himself, so he projected this desire onto his wife in order to justify his behavior.

Projection works just like a movie projector that puts forth an image on the screen. We put our forbidden self on the movie screen of our mate's psyche, and thus we see our lost parts portrayed or enacted by someone else. This gets us off the hook from owning and healing our own stuff. It also allows us to continue hiding or repressing our real feelings. It is safe to say then that we project onto our partner that which we fear seeing within ourselves. When a problem arises in marriage, our tendency is to look outside of our own psyches, and project blame onto our spouses. This may blind us from seeing our own insecurities.

Projections Take the Form of Anger

The main way we project our own insecurities onto our partner is through anger. Anger is usually the way our mate retaliates as well. We will either become furious with our spouse for possessing the same behaviors that we despise in ourselves or furious with ourselves for our own dark side. Often, we become angry because we know our partner's criticisms have a morsel of truth, but we do not want to accept it. In order to deflect their disparagement, we become angry and project. This is what we did in our marriage.

I became angry with Tom because I felt that he was too frivolous. He became angry with me because he thought that I was too frugal. What I was afraid to see was my own insecurities about being out of control. Tom was afraid to examine his insecurities about feeling inadequate. Projecting these insecurities onto each other gave us the perfect excuse not to look inside. Our projections typically took the form of anger.

Our anger was not really the main problem, however. In fact, anger is more of the reaction to, rather than the root of, a particular situation. Psychoanalytic theory teaches us that anger is really a secondary response to four basic primary emotions that are actually present when a person gets upset. These emotions are guilt, inferiority or inadequacy, fear, and trauma or pain. Most people have a hard time remembering these roots of rage, much less expressing them. In order to help people remember these core issues and get in touch with what was at the heart of their anger we developed this acronym and put it in the form of an exercise. It is called The GIFT Exercise.

THE GIFT EXERCISE

When you are feeling angry, instead of just getting mad and projecting that anger onto your partner, stop for a moment and think about what that anger is really about. Attach it to one of these basic emotions that cause you to feel insecure and respond in anger.

> **G**uilt
> **I**nferiority/Inadequacy
> **F**ear
> **T**rauma or Pain

The acronym for these roots of anger spell the word GIFT. We thought that it was very appropriate, because it is a gift to your marriage to discuss the root rather than the rage. As you attach a primary feeling to your anger, express this feeling to your spouse rather than just telling them that you are mad. When you tell your partner about what is upsetting you, use the format, "When you ... I feel ...."

An example might be, "When you are late and you don't call, I feel fear that something has happened to you." This format is so much more conducive to conflict resolution than saying something such as, "You make me so mad because you are so inconsiderate when you don't call."

Bev and I learned to use The GIFT Exercise to discuss our anger. It made it so much easier for us to remember what was at the root of our rage and express it. The GIFT also helped us not to provoke or falsely accuse each other. It was also hard to project our own insecurities onto each other when we used this exercise because it enabled us to get in touch with what we were really feeling. This exercise can be helpful for all couples, but we found that it is has really been a healing balm for ACODPs, who tend to have bountiful insecurities as a result of the demise of their families. We tell ACODPs to try this exercise when insecurities surface, and they will see that it is better to communicate than infuriate.

YOUR GIFT EXERCISE

Now, take a situation that makes you mad at your partner. Get in touch with the root of your rage. Use the acronym GIFT to remember the core issues that cause anger. They are Guilt, Inferiority, Fear or Trauma. Then, express this root to your partner, using the "When you … I feel …" format. If it helps you to communicate better, write down what you are going to say before you confront your spouse. This will help you better understand yourself and your mate. It will also help you to express yourself more constructively.

Chapter 7

The Inability-to-Communicate Wound

Fred and Ginger had been married for twelve years. They had two children, ages two and four. Both of them were adult children of divorced parents. Ginger's dad decided after thirty years of marriage that he wanted to leave and pursue a relationship with an old high school sweetheart. Ginger's mother was so depressed that she had to be hospitalized. This caused Ginger to quit college to come home and take care of her mother. Ginger lived with her mom for three years to help Mom get back on her feet. It was a hard time for Ginger because her mom was miserable and bitter and very negative about her dad, and men in general.

During this time Ginger met Fred, a young graduate student at the local university, and they fell in love. This upset mom who was not only really jealous of the time they spent together but also upset that Ginger did not heed her warning that all men were bad. Ginger's mom had nothing positive to say about men. Fred was no exception. Mom barraged Ginger with a slew of disapproving comments about Fred. She said things such as, "He's a man, so he can't be trusted. He will abandon you. All men are weak and give in to temptation too easily. They will eventually stray from marriage." This caused Ginger to get cold feet anytime Fred talked about the future. She even broke up with him once because of the pressure her mother put on her and the fear that resulted from all Mom's negative programming.

Fred was sympathetic and encouraged Ginger to stay in the relationship and work things out. He had a special understanding of what she was going through because his parents had divorced when he was nine years old. His dad also ran away with another woman, leaving his mother distraught and depressed. After his dad left, things were very tight financially so his mom went back to work. Fred and his two older brothers took care of each other and the house while mom worked. Mom would come home tired and depressed. Typically, she would take out her frustrations on Fred and his brothers. She would criticize how they cooked and cleaned. This made Fred feel like nothing he ever did was good enough for his mom. He felt that after the divorce he, in some ways, had lost both of his parents.

Both Fred and Ginger felt the negative effects of their parents' divorces. It took a long time for them to feel comfortable enough to get married. Ginger had a lot of trust issues, and Fred said that he despised the feeling of being the kid in the neighborhood who was fatherless and had trouble making ends meet financially. All of his friends had dads who took them on vacations and bought them things. Fred said that when he grew up that he was going to make a lot of money and provide for his family in a way his father never did.

Robert Lewis, founder of the Men's Fraternity and author of *Raising a Modern-Day Knight*, says that men who are raised without fathers have a slow, seething, suppressed rage. This slow-boiling anger was a problem for Fred. Often, Ginger was the target.

Despite their issues, Fred and Ginger made a commitment to marriage, hoping that all of the problems of their parents' divorces would not trouble them. They were naïve about how these concerns could plague them until they found themselves stuck and unable to resolve certain conflicts in their marriage. They did pretty well until they hit their toxic subjects, the difficult subjects in marriage that are tough to resolve. At these times, they could not communicate with each other. They came into counseling because they were very frustrated and did not know to resolve these differences.

Toxic Subjects

Toxic subjects are those areas in marriage that cause the greatest amount of conflict. The most common toxic subjects in marriage are money, sex, in-laws, jealousy for time spent outside the marriage, roles, and childrearing. One of Fred and Ginger's toxic subjects was their inability to strike a balance of roles in caring for the children.

Ginger worked part-time in sales and Fred worked for a large architectural firm. Ginger felt like all of the responsibilities for raising and caring for their two small children always fell on her. Fred felt that he worked hard and deserved to relax some when he came home. The evenings were stressful for them because they had to prepare dinner, feed the children, bathe them, and put them to bed. Ginger wanted Fred to help more, and Fred thought that Ginger nagged too much and was too critical.

Fred and Ginger also had in-law troubles. To add to their stress, Ginger's mother usually called every evening around dinnertime, and Ginger felt like she needed to be there for her mom because she was her mom's main support. Fred resented her long phone conversations. He said that Ginger would rather spend time talking to her mother than being with him. Ginger felt responsible for her mother because she watched as she suffered from the divorce. Unfortunately, Mom reinforced this by expecting Ginger to be her caretaker.

Another toxic subject for Fred and Ginger was sex. Fred was frustrated because their sex life was suffering, due to the fact that Ginger said that she was so tired every night. Ginger was annoyed with Fred because he seemed to want sex all of the time. He had become critical of her as a sexual partner, often commenting on how little they made love, or how tired and cold she was. Ginger countered by saying that if Fred would just help more around the house maybe she would not be so tired. They could not communicate about the toxic subjects of childcare, in-laws, and sex. Problems in these areas went unresolved and the tension between them continued to build.

Fred and Ginger needed help. While many of these conflicts are normal for all couples and not indigenous to ACODPs, it became clear to us that part of their difficulty in communicating their issues was *because* they were ACODPs. Ginger was afraid to bring up thorny issues because she feared it would make Fred want to leave like her father did. She stuffed her feelings and would not tell Fred how she really felt or what she needed for fear that he would abandon her.

Fred said that his father's leaving and subsequent absence caused him to want to work hard to make money so his family would not have to do without. Because of this, he was overly committed to work. He gave so much energy at his job that he had little left over for Ginger and the kids. When Ginger would comment about this, he would become very defensive, saying that she did not appreciate how hard he worked and that he was doing it all for his family. Ginger had trouble believing this, because his overworking seemed to be hurting his family, not helping it. When these toxic issues surfaced, they could not reach an understanding. It seems that their parents' divorces were haunting them still.

Ginger felt overwhelmed and Fred felt unappreciated. These were the exact same feelings that they had as a result of their parents' divorces. Because their soul wounds were being tapped into, they made up their own realities about each other, based on these soul wounds. They perceived each other negatively because they were seeing each other through the negative filters of their families-of-origin. Their parents' divorces clouded these filters. The harmful perceptions caused them to draw false conclusions about each other's motives. Fred and Ginger were in a power struggle.

Power Struggle

We define a power struggle as a situation in which there is an underlying tension that is characterized by fear, which results in a breakdown in communication that leads to assumptions. In a power struggle, a couple typically assumes the worst about each other. The soul wounds a person experiences often become the theme of their negative assumptions. These harmful suppositions can be based on childhood introjections, rather than the actual reality.

Ginger and Fred experienced an underlying tension in their marriage. This tension was laced with fear. Ginger feared that all of the work and responsibility in caring for the children was going to fall on her shoulders. She was also afraid that Fred did not really care about her. This caused her to assume things about him like he was selfish, lazy, and uncaring. Her negative mindset made her actually look for behaviors in Fred that would define him as selfish and uncaring.

Fred feared that no matter what he did for Ginger, it would not be good enough. He made up the reality that Ginger was a hard-to-please nag. He thought that she was negative and critical like his mother. This made him actually look for any behavior in Ginger that might be interpreted that way.

If someone looks for something long enough, they will find it, even if they have to project that it exists. We have noticed that if an individual starts to look for certain behaviors in their spouse, it is easy to interpret their partner's actions according to what they are looking for. In other words, "you will see that which you want to see." This is because you are looking through the eyes of fear. Fear is a very powerful motivator. Many times, a person's greatest fear can actually happen because they unconsciously participate in a self-fulfilling prophecy to bring it about.

The book of Job in the Old Testament tells the story of the man, Job, who actually watched as his greatest fears came upon him. The part he played in bringing this about was being so fearful that he actually walked in the direction of his fear. Job's fear and worry consumed him causing him to become obsessed with the possibility that they may happen. Because he focused on this possible calamity so much, he unconsciously contributed to it taking place. He created his own self-fulfilling prophecy. The saying, "As a man thinks, so he is," really applied here. Fred and Ginger did the same thing when they projected their childhood fears onto each other. Both of them were, in fact, ushering in their worst fears. Like the character Job, their lack of faith in each other and in their relationship was causing their fears to be realities.

Fred and Ginger were seeing only the bad in their relationship. Their fear would not let them see the good. Many of these negative assumptions that Fred and Ginger made about each other were rooted in their childhood fears as ACODPs, and they were re-injuring each other in much the same way as they each were injured in their families-of-origin.

Communication Breakdown

Projecting these fears onto each other caused Fred and Ginger's communication to break down. This was just one more downward step in their difficult power struggle. Things would be all right for a while and then one of them would feel slighted or overwhelmed. They would have a conflict, get really upset, and then withdraw from each other. At that point they would stop talking, and this drove a wedge between them. Both of them felt hurt and uncared for. They knew that resentment was building between them, but they blamed this on each other. Their ACODP issues of fear and insecurity were causing the ship of their marriage to slowly sink. Fred and Ginger had to learn how to communicate with one another and to resolve their toxic issues.

Connecting the Present to the Past

First, they had to see the part their parents' divorces played in their inability to communicate and resolve conflict. The IGMP Exercise helped them see how they had internalized, generalized, and maximized issues because they were reminders of their past. As Ginger did her IGMP Exercise she determined her life theme. She believed that, "You can't count on the people you love to come through for you." Ginger wanted to finish the exercise by pulverizing her fears, but she couldn't because Fred was triggering them in their relationship. Fred was re-injuring her the same way that she was wounded in her family-of-origin.

Triggering these fears caused Ginger to be very overwhelmed with the responsibility of caring for the children. This feeling replicated what she experienced after her parents' divorce and she was left to care for her depressed mother. When Fred would balk at helping her in the evenings with the household chores, she had old brainers about being overwhelmed and alone, with too much responsibility. Her old brainers triggered her reactivity and she overreacted to Fred.

Her response to Fred triggering her soul wounds was similar to the response she had in childhood and early adulthood after her parents divorced. First, she tried to say how she felt about being overwhelmed. She would try to coerce and manipulate others into helping. Then, she would give up and withdraw. In her withdrawal, Ginger would pout and become cold and aloof. This is exactly what she did in her relationship with Fred. We have noticed that adults respond to their old brainers similarly to the way they did in childhood.

When Fred did his IGMP Exercise he determined his life theme as well. He had an internal belief that, "No matter what I do, it will never be good enough." This feeling came from his childhood when his mother would get mad at him for not caring for the house and doing his chores while she was working. His mother's nagging and criticism caused him to feel inadequate, inferior, and alone. This is exactly what he felt with Ginger. Like her, he wanted to finish the IGMP Exercise and pulverize his fears, but he couldn't because Ginger was triggering them so much in the marriage. Ginger was wounding Fred like his mother did. This was why he was so reactive.

In Fred's reactivity, he would become angry and defensive and list all that he did around the house. Once he saw that she was not buying his argument, he would withdraw from Ginger physically and emotionally. He usually went to his study and watched television to get away from Ginger. This is also what he had done in his childhood. When mom would nag and criticize him, he would just go to his room and stay there.

We saw that Fred and Ginger were replicating each other's ACODP wounds from their families-of-origin. We also determined that they were adapting to these wounds in the same way they had as children. People usually carry their unhealthy adaptation patterns with them into adulthood. These harmful responses to wounds did not help them in childhood, and they were not aiding in resolving their conflicts as adults either. We tell couples that, "If nothing changes, then nothing changes." This means that in order for their marriage to improve, they could not continue doing the same things they had always done. To change their behavior, they had to understand themselves and each other. They had to take the steps to understanding and change.

Steps to Understanding and Change

1. Couples have to dig deeper into their psyches and identify triggers in their current relationship and understand the feelings these triggers evoke. In doing this, they will see that they are displaying reactivity to the old brainers that are being triggered in their marriage. A great deal of this reactivity is the result of their parents' divorces.
2. They have to attach those feelings to childhood wounds and separate family-of-origin issues from patterns in their marriage.
3. They need to see how they react when their old brainers are being triggered in their current relationship. Typically, their behaviors are similar to what they exhibited in childhood.
4. They need to determine what they really need in their marriage.

5. They must learn how to communicate this need in a healthy way to each other.

We have developed a concise, easy-to-do technique that organizes the above actions so that couples can better accomplish them. This tool helps couples understand each other's soul wounds, see how childhood introjections affect their present behavior, and enable them to change their negative behaviors. This process aids them in healing old patterns and developing new ones in their marriage. We introduced this technique to Fred and Ginger. The technique is called The Digging Deeper Exercise.

THE DIGGING DEEPER EXERCISE

This exercise consists of five basic steps that we have developed, which will simplify the process of expressing frustration and anger in your relationships. We stumbled onto this tool while dealing with our own frustrations in our marriage. You will be amazed at how much smoother conflict is resolved by using this tool. In order to work through the steps, you need to answer the following questions:

1. **What is the behavior that my mate does that triggers my anger?**
   When my mate does this ... I feel this ....
2. **Identify the root of this anger using The GIFT Exercise.**
3. **When have I ever felt this feeling before?**
4. **What do I do when feel I this feeling? What is my behavior?**
5. **What do I really need?**

Requirement Equals Resistance

In our soul-healing love model, we have a saying that, "Requirement equals resistance." If you require something, if you make it mandatory, people will resist doing it more than if you gave them the freedom of choice. This frustrating aspect of human behavior is troublesome for marriage, but it is as old as the story of Adam and Eve in the garden of Eden. In the Genesis account of paradise, Adam and Eve could have anything to eat that they wanted. There was only one food that was prohibited, the fruit of the tree of the knowledge of good and evil. This prohibition made them want it all the more.

If you have a hard time accepting this generalization, think about this. Let's say that your neighbor picks up your paper and places it on your porch every afternoon by five o'clock. You are very grateful for his thoughtfulness. But then one day you walk over and tell him that you are coming home early and you want him to bring your paper in at three o'clock instead of five. Do you honestly think that your neighbor will oblige you? We think not. The requirement you placed on him will cause him to resist your request. When you take away your neighbor's free will, he will be more likely to withstand your appeal. This has been human nature since the garden of Eden.

Fred and Ginger's requirements for each other were met with resistance as well. Ginger wanted Fred to help more. Fred wanted Ginger to back off more. If they met each other's needs, then they would surely not get their own needs met. Fred and Ginger were at a stalemate and would not budge to assist each other. In their power struggle, neither one of them was willing to give up their position. Fred and Ginger had to find a way to understand each other's needs in a different context so that they could respond to them. They had to see each other's needs in the context of their childhood wounds and their issues as ACODPs.

Unmet Needs in the Power Struggle

The fears that people have and project onto each other are associated with their unmet needs. The fact that these needs weren't met creates fear that they will not be met again. When this fear is tapped into, reactivity occurs. This reactivity centers on the trigger. This is what happened to Fred and Ginger. This is why they could never get beyond the power struggle. They responded to their triggers in a fight-or-flight manner. Doing this never gave them an opportunity to understand why they were being reactive. It also never gave their partner a chance to empathize with their reactivity, much less meet their needs.

The Digging Deeper Exercise gives couples the opportunity to do all of the above. It allows them to go to the dark place of fear and unmet needs in their psyches, without so much apprehension. Because people resist visiting painful places in their psyches, it becomes easier for them to project, attribute, or blame that fear onto each other. This only exacerbates the power struggle. The Digging Deeper Exercise allows couples to understand and empathize with the deepest fears in each other and work toward communicating and resolving them.

Guidelines and Stipulations

There are a few provisions that we stipulate in doing The Digging Deeper Exercise. We gave these conditions to Fred and Ginger as well. First, couples are to practice intentionality, the ability to act in a healing way despite their reactivity. Second, they are to be safe for each other. This means that they must welcome each other's sharing and not use it against one another in the future. Third, they need to treat the information they receive from each other as very special, even sacred. It takes a lot to be vulnerable, especially with your spouse whom you presume to be an intimate enemy at times. In order for this vulnerability to be well received, it must be treated with utmost respect and empathy. Fred and Ginger worked hard to meet these requirements. They were then ready to do their Digging Deeper Exercises and compare their answers.

GINGER'S DIGGING DEEPER EXERCISE

1. **What is the behavior that my mate does that triggers my anger?**

   When my mate does this ... I feel this ....

   When Fred does not help me with the chores around the house and with the children, I feel overwhelmed, unimportant, and uncared for.

2. **Identify the root of this anger using The GIFT Exercise.**

   The roots of my anger are Inferiority and Trauma.

3. **When have I ever felt this feeling before?**

   I felt these feelings when my parents divorced and I was left with too much responsibility.

4. **What do I do when feel I this feeling? What is my behavior?**

I get angry and accuse, coerce, and manipulate to get help.
When this does not work, I pout and withdraw. I become cold
and aloof.

5. **What do I really need?**

Until I did this exercise, I thought that I just needed for Fred to
stop being selfish with his time and simply help me. Now, I
realize that my need is much deeper. I now see that I need for
Fred to let me know that he understands how overwhelmed I was
after my parents' divorce, and how he is causing me to relive
this with him. I need to know that I am important enough to him
for him to help me.

FRED'S DIGGING DEEPER EXERCISE

1. **What is the behavior that my mate does that triggers my anger?**

When my mate does this ... I feel this ....

When Ginger criticizes and nags me, I feel like nothing I do is
ever good enough for her.

2. **Identify the root of this anger using The GIFT Exercise.**

I feel Inferiority and Trauma.

3. **When have I ever felt this feeling before?**

I felt these feelings as a child, when my parents divorced and I
was left to care for things, and my mother criticized my efforts.
I would try hard to please her, but it never seemed to work.

4. **What do I do when feel I this feeling? What is my behavior?**

I get angry and defensive, and start listing all the things that I
have done to help. When this does not work, I withdraw.

5. **What do I really need?**

Before this exercise, I would have said that I needed for Ginger
to get off my back, and quit nagging. Now, I realize that my
needs are less superficial and much more profound. I need for
Ginger to think that I am good enough and adequate as a person,
husband, and father, and to verbally affirm me.

Digging Deeper Changes Requirements

Before completing The Digging Deeper Exercise, Fred and Ginger found their needs to be surface and shallow. They basically just wanted their way. Ginger simply wanted Fred to help her more. Fred just wanted her to get off his back. Their resistance was killing their marriage. After completing their Digging Deeper Exercises, they both realized that their needs were much deeper. Ginger wanted to feel understood and cared for, and Fred wanted to feel appreciated for his contributions. Neither of their needs were unrealistic. Neither wanted something from their mate that was impossible to give. In fact, meeting each other's needs actually could heal their ACODP wounds, the very wounds that had plagued them their whole lives. Their mates had the power to wound them, but they also had an amazing power to heal them as well.

The Power to Heal

This power to heal is awesome in marriage and should be treated as a sacred gift. We call this power soul-healing love, because it can heal the wounded soul of your partner as it heals your own. In order to tap into this power to heal, couples have to see that their very behaviors are re-injuring each other in destructive ways. As many ACODPs see this, they are motivated to change. Many of them have said to us that even though they are hurting each other, they indeed do not want to wound their partners like they were wounded in childhood. Even in difficult marriages, most couples do not intentionally want to hurt one another. Fred and Ginger were no exception.

Both Fred and Ginger saw that they were re-wounding each other. They realized that they were replicating each other's wounds as ACODPs. This insight enabled them to move toward healing. We asked Fred a very important question. "Fred, if you knew that your helping more in the evenings with the children would not only send a message to Ginger that you indeed cared for her but also begin to heal a wound from her parents' divorce, would you be willing to do this? "Yes," Fred replied, without hesitation.

We asked Ginger, "If you knew that verbally appreciating Fred for the things he does do around the house, instead of pointing out the things he does not do, would not only make him feel that he was good enough for you but also heal his inadequacy wound from his parents' divorce, would you be willing to do this? "Absolutely," cried Ginger.

Both Fred and Ginger were eager to meet each other's needs once they saw them in a different context. Instead of seeing each other as selfish and demanding, they saw each other as wounded, and in need of love and care. This new vision of each other as wounded ACODPs, not self-centered, difficult mates, motivated them to really want to meet each other's needs. This fresh image of each other motivated them to make changes in their relationship. Fred was more willing to help with the chores and Ginger willingly offered verbal praise.

"Want To" or Desire Is Healing

As Fred and Ginger set out on their healing journey they were inspired to make things better in their marriage. They purposed to heal each other and were very motivated to make things work. If you think that everything went wonderful after that you must remember they are still human. Do you think that Fred jumped up to help Ginger every time she needed him? Do you think that Ginger enthusiastically expressed appreciation for Fred every time he helped? The answer to these questions is a resounding "no." Fred and Ginger could not do everything perfectly ten out of ten times, all the time.

So how did Fred and Ginger get healed? The answer lies in their desire. After completing The Digging Deeper Exercise, both Fred and Ginger knew that they did not want to hurt each other. Both of them knew that they actually wanted to heal each other. This desire to be a healing agent was the salve they needed to begin their healing.

In a counseling session shortly after Fred and Ginger finished their Digging Deeper Exercise, we asked Ginger if Fred always helped every time she needed him. Ginger smiled and said, "Of course not." " Then why are you not upset with him?" we questioned. Ginger made a very important statement. She said, "Fred does not help every time I need him, but I am not upset like I used to be, because this time I know in my soul that he *really wants* to. It's just that sometimes, things get in the way." Ginger knew Fred's desire was to support her and heal her. Previously, she had attributed motives to Fred that were destructive. Now that she saw him through new eyes, she could see that he really did want to be a good husband. He really did want to heal her. His "want to" made all of the difference in how she viewed him.

The fact that both Fred and Ginger wanted to be healing agents for each other covered a multitude of sins that they committed in their relationship. This "want to" gave them the grace to heal each other's souls. It can do so for you as well.

YOUR DIGGING DEEPER EXERCISE

Take this time to complete your Digging Deeper Exercise. List several frustrations that you have toward your spouse and have them list their frustrations toward you. Answer all of the questions before you go to the next trigger. Share your answers with each other and learn to see each other through different eyes.

1. **What is the behavior that my mate does that triggers my anger?**
   When my mate does this ... I feel this ....
2. **Identify the root of this anger using The GIFT Exercise.**
3. **When have I ever felt this feeling before?**
4. **What do I do when feel I this feeling? What is my behavior?**
5. **What do I really need?**

Chapter 8

Social Structure Wounds

Social structure is defined as your societal or community composition. It is also your collective cultural construction or formation. Adult children of divorced parents have a wounded social structure in many ways. Their societal composition has been fractured. For example, ACODPs have no mentors for marriage, no examples of healthy communication or problem solving. ACODPs have severed relationships. They lose contact with family, friends, and relatives. They can have problems with their extended families and in-laws as result of this disconnection.

ACODPs have loyalty issues that affect their social structure. They feel disloyal and guilty when getting close to one side of the family in lieu of the other. ACODPs can lose touch with their communities. This happens when they have to move as a result of divorce or when they have to choose between parents in different locations.

We saw in Chapter 1 that divorce weakens the structure of society at large, in that it deteriorates the religious life of a family, contributes to delinquency and criminality, and increases the possibility of drug and alcohol abuse. ACODPs and our culture as a whole suffer from these scars and need help in healing them.

Lack of a Marriage Mentor

As a result of their parents' divorces, ACODPs often travel the roads of marriage without a compass. They truly mirror Judith Wallerstein's statement that, "They have no internal image of a relationship as it moves through the years." They have no examples to help them learn the ropes of marriage. This lack of a marriage mentor wound creates mistrust between parents and their adult children and their communication can be stilted. Both Tom and I never went to either set of parents for relationship advice. We simply could not trust their track record in marriage.

We attended a small Christian university on the west coast. Many of our fellow students came from the lineage of great Christian orators, famous theologians, and pillars of the church. We were the only people in our group of friends who came from divorced homes. We watched in envy as they planned their weddings and learned the ropes of new married life from their gracious teachers, who also happened to be their parents. It seemed that even planning their weddings went smoother. We would sit in awe listening to the stories that they would tell us of how their parents gave them wonderful advice about marriage. "Wow," we thought, "what must this be like to have the support and tutelage of happy, healthy married parents?" We will never know. This truly saddened us.

The lack of mentors for marriage takes its toll on a young married couple. Without mentors, there is a huge hole in their social structure. There is also a subtle feeling deep within them that if their parents did not make it perhaps they can't either. Hearing that the statistics are stacked against them causes fear as well. It is hard for them to think that they will be the couple that can beat the odds. Without good marital examples, it can seem hopeless at times.

Finding a Mentor: The Story of Us

Tom and I entered marriage with a great deal of hope that was laced with fear and trepidation. The feeling that the other shoe was going to drop haunted us continually. It was particularly difficult when we got into a struggle. We had no idea how to fight fairly or resolve conflict. In my home, the marital disagreements usually turned violent. In Tom's home, they could not resolve issues so that both parties could feel cared for and satisfied. Their final solution to solving their problems was dissolution. Tom learned to give up. I learned to avoid conflict in order to avert disaster. Both of the methods of problem solving that we learned from our families-of-origin were extremely unhealthy. Consequently, when we got into an argument, we did not know what to do. We couldn't call home. We could not ask our parents for advice, and we couldn't trust the unsolicited advice that was offered. We were lost. Those early days of marital adjustment evoked a lot of feelings of hopelessness within us.

We shared with you in earlier chapters about how we took classes, read books, and attended seminars on marriage. They were all helpful, but they were no substitute for dealing with our fears, wounds, and insecurities head on. They are, however, helpful as you resolve your fears so that you can learn specific tools and techniques to building a better marriage. During the beginning years of our marriage, there were only a few marriage education programs around. The Catholic Church had Pre-Cana classes for engaged couples. David and Vera Mace started The Association for Couples in Marriage Enrichment, a couples' training and support group for marriage. We soaked up these experiences. They were key in helping us learn healthy ways of interacting as a couple. Since that time, there have been many wonderful marriage education and skills training groups that have been formed in this country and internationally. Several well-known universities have researched what makes couples healthy, and have put together marriage skills programs that are available across the country. These programs share with couples the results of their research. They are teaching people what healthy couples do to make their marriages last. Marriage-mentoring programs are sprouting up in churches and parishes all over the country. This is indeed the age for marriage, and we are thrilled about it.

We are envious of today's couples because they have so many resources at their fingertips. Today's ACODPs need not be troubled by the fact that they do not have parents who can be constructive marriage mentors. Now, there are a plethora of resources for them to choose from. With the dawn of the internet, these resources can become available at the click of a button. Just visit ACODP.com to check out a list of resources for building healthy relationships.

When we realized that we did not have qualified mentors for marriage, one of the things that saved us was seeking advisors who were outside of our family. Since we were going to a Christian university there were several wonderful professors and administrators who were good models of solid married couples. We watched their examples and listened to their recommendations. We encourage ACODPs to find mentor couples. You can do this through a formal marriage-mentoring program in your parish, church, synagogue, or community or informally as Tom and I did. Find a couple who can be real with you and allow you to share with them. Watch them. Study their interactions. Learn from their relationship issues and follow their examples.

One particular couple that meant a great deal to us was married for more than thirty years when we met them. We will never forget David and Eloise. The thing that stood out to us was that they genuinely liked each other. They were very real and not syrupy sweet, but they sincerely cared for one another. They let us ask questions and share our struggles, and always they listened and did not judge. They never took sides, though sometimes, we must admit, we wanted them to. They always took the side of the marriage. Without them ever saying it, we could tell that they believed in marriage. In the age of convenient divorces, they genuinely believed in marriage, and what was even better, they believed in *our* marriage. Sometimes they believed when we did not even have the faith to believe in it ourselves. They were a rare gift to us and to our marriage.

One day while eating with them, we asked David and Eloise to share with us their greatest marital strengths. "She is my companion and my best friend," said David. Eloise echoed his sentiment and said, "David is my best friend too, and there is nothing I wouldn't do for him and he for me."

I still remember talking with this amiable couple about their marriage. As we were sharing, David left the room for a moment. Without blinking, Eloise said, "Bring me one, too." Tom and I looked at each other with bewilderment. "Bring me what?" I asked. Before Eloise could answer me, David walked in the room with two glasses of iced tea. "Here you are, darlin', your tea, just like you asked for it."

"Thank you, dear," she replied sweetly.

"Wait a minute," I said to David. "Eloise didn't ask for anything. How did you know what she wanted? She just said 'bring me one, too' as you left the room."

They both looked at me somewhat puzzled, and David asked us, "Didn't she ask for that tea? I could have sworn she asked."

"No," I said, "She didn't say a word."

As they both began to chuckle, David calmly replied, "Oh well, I guess we were reading each other's minds again. We do this all the time now. We communicate so well, I guess we forget to use words." David and Eloise continued sharing about their marriage as if nothing incredible had just happened. For them it wasn't incredible. It was natural. They had developed the natural ability to anticipate each other's needs. David knowingly said, "We tell our grown kids that this mind-reading stuff doesn't come easy. They've got to learn it like mom and I did. We didn't always know what each other wanted, we had to get it by watchin,' and just bein' around each other. We got it by carin.' You just can't start off like this; it takes years to develop."

We asked David and Eloise what motivated them to keep trying until they got it right. Without hesitation, they said in unison, "Want to." "Want to? What is that?" Tom inquired. Meaningfully, David responded, "You gotta want to with all of your heart even when is doesn't come naturally. That just about says it all." David and Eloise had been practicing intentionality, the art of "faking it till you make it," and they didn't even know it. They had mastered the art of doing what ever it takes to be healthy no matter how you feel. We felt privileged to be a part of that sacred moment between these long-term, married sages. It gave us hope for our marriage as we learned to develop some "want to" of our own.

Repeated studies of happily married couples echo what David and Eloise told us that day. Long-term, married couples who have happy marriages say that the single most important ingredient in their marriage is friendship. The majority of the couples surveyed said that their mate was their best friend. The results of one significant study done by

Jeanette and Robert Lauer and published in *Psychology Today*, showed that friendship was the most significant factor in healthy, happy, long-term couples, winning over mutual political beliefs, similar financial styles, passion, and sexual fulfillment. Building friendship means learning to trust and overcome fear. We have already seen that this can be a challenge for adult children of divorced parents. This is why we need mentors to show us the way.

Severed Relationships

After a divorce, individuals tend to lose contact with their in-laws, certain family friends, and co-workers of their spouse. Many of their friends, co-workers, and in-laws tend to "pick sides" so that there are broken relationships. This not only affects the adults who are divorcing but it also causes a great deal of pain for the children as well, especially in adulthood. Divorce often strains or completely severs the child's relationship with at least one parent, often the father. Some ACODPs then lose track of whole sides of their family. If a parent moves away, they may lose contact with that parents' family because there is no one to see that they stay in touch. Some custodial parents forbid their children to associate with their ex-spouse's family. This break in family relationships is very damaging to the social structure of adult children of divorced parents. ACODPs carry the scars of these shattered relationships for a long time.

Bev's Story

Perhaps one of the greatest pains that I suffered from my parents' divorce was the loss of close family friends and relatives. My mother and father became bitter enemies. They did not speak to each other, nor did they speak kindly about each other to us children. My mother was the main custodial parent and she forbade me to see my father's family. I was not allowed to see my grandmother or my aunts and uncles. Since I was only five years old when my parents divorced I did not know any of my dad's family very well. This meant that there was a whole side of my family that I could never really get to know. This was so unfair, but I was the pleaser, so I complied.

As I grew up, I started to realize that I had an entire heritage that I knew very little about. As I tried to spend time with them and get to know my roots, I felt left out, like an outsider. Family reunions were awkward. Funerals were the worst, trying to grieve the loss of someone that I never knew. Consequently, I found reasons that I could not attend. I felt like I just didn't fit in. I even picked a university three thousand miles away from both sides of the family. I now realize that I was looking for a geographic cure for the misplaced feelings that plagued me. These severed relationships saddened me, but I think they did even more damage. They caused me to sever relationships in my own life too quickly and easily. I kept my distance from people, fearing that if I really let them get to know me, they would not like me. I had a great deal of emotional cutoff.

Emotional Cutoff

Transgenerational family therapist Murray Bowen coined the term "emotional cutoff" to describe family systems that were distant and disengaged. He contrasted disengaged families to families that valued connection and closeness which he called "enmeshed" families. He found that enmeshed families were very entangled and could be unhealthy in that respect, but that they had very little emotional cutoff. Individuals that suffer from emotional cutoff have trouble with intimacy. They fear closeness and tend to devalue relationships, so they do not easily get close to others.

My family system was very disengaged. This made me hard-to-get-to-know and distant in relationships. I was afraid to get close to people because I was afraid that I would lose contact with them, much like I did with my father and his family. Selecting a college so far away ensured that I would not get too close to the friends and family that I had at home and I also could not get too close to the friends that I made at school. I was always just distant enough from everyone to play it safe.

Unfortunately, I was always lonely and did not know why. On the surface, it looked like I had loads of friends on both coasts. But inside, I craved connection and bonding. I wanted to belong and did not feel like I fit in anywhere. This was a result of the scars of being an adult child of divorced parents and I reviled it. Emotional cutoff is a problem for ACODPs, which is one of the reasons that they seem to be able to end marriages more frequently than adult children from intact families. Unconsciously, they carry with them the belief that relationships do not last. This can be deadly and destructive for their emotional well-being, their social structure, and their marriages.

Tom's Story

Bev was not the only one who struggled with emotional cutoff as a result of her parents' divorce. I had my share of distancing also. When my parents divorced, I was very angry at my dad. So angry in fact that I did not speak to him for more than two years. Some of my anger was because of his chronic adultery and how it destroyed my family. But some of my rage was because of the things my dad said about my mom. Obviously, my dad's family was going to defend him and I just could not agree with them. This broke my family apart. My sister and I did not see my dad or his side of the family for many years. The breach was so great that neither dad nor his family came to our wedding. It was so sad for me not to be able to share this part of my life with them.

The estrangement from my father's mother, my sweet Portuguese grandmother, was particularly hard for me because we were so close growing up. We had a special bond that was fractured after my parents' divorce. I loved my grandma very much. She was from Portugal and cooked Portuguese dishes that I still crave today. I had great memories of spending time with her and with my aunts, uncles, and cousins on holidays. All of this stopped after the divorce. I was lost. To deal with my pain, I put a shield around me to protect myself. Unlike Bev, I wasn't gracious. I was distant and suspicious. I vowed that I would never get hurt again and to do that I would not get too close. This emotional cutoff followed me much of my early adult life. It even negatively affected me in my vocation.

Here I was a pastor, wanting desperately to get close to people, and all the while fighting this unhealthy distancing mechanism that haunted me. It is a wonder that Bev and I got together at all. Our meeting, and subsequent mating, made me think that God definitely had something to do with this because we could never have done this on our own with the amount of emotional cutoff we both possessed from our parents' divorces.

Thank goodness we had the wisdom to connect and fight the curses that were left to us as a result of our severed relationships from divorce. Loss of family is not the only damage that ACODPs suffer. They can lose contact with meaningful family friends that cause them a great deal of pain as well.

George and Gracey's Story

Several years ago we treated a young couple, George and Gracey, who had been married six months. Incidentally, they had invited George's dad's business partner to their wedding. George had not seen this man since his parents' divorce, some fifteen years prior. He remembered scenes of going on family vacations with dad's partner and his wife and they were very good times for him. After George's parents divorced, he never saw dad's business partner again. There were no more trips to his lake house, no more outings on his houseboat, and no more connection. George went out on a limb and invited his dad's partner to his wedding. When they were reunited at the wedding, George was overwhelmed with emotions that took him by surprise. He was so overcome with feelings that he could not stop crying. This was not only embarrassing for him, to be seen crying profusely at his own wedding, but it was also very painful. He did not realize that he had such deep grief about the loss of this man's friendship. As he started to grieve this loss, he saw other losses that troubled him as a result of his parents' divorce.

Loyalty Issues

Adult children of divorced parents have severe loyalty issues. If they are loyal to one side of the family, this usually means that they are disloyal to the other. A reunion with one side of the family usually means parting with the other side, and vice versa. As one of our clients put it, " When you're a child of divorce, you are always missing and hurting someone. If you spend time with one family member, the other is absent. There is always a sense of longing."

Bev's Story

This feeling of longing was one of the greatest pains that I suffered as an adult child of divorced parents. Indeed, I was always missing somebody. This longing created a feeling of disloyalty to the parent that I was missing. This disloyalty resulted in a great deal of guilt. I felt guilty when I was with one parent because I could not be with the other. My parents fed this guilt by acting pitiful when I would leave to visit the other parent, or by asking me to choose between the two of them for vacations and holidays. These feeling of disloyalty and guilt just about buried me. I walked around most of my life feeling overly responsible for their feelings and guilty for hurting them with my disloyalty.

I even felt guilty at family reunions and special family gatherings. As an adult, I chose to spend time getting to know my father's family. Every time I was with them, I felt this internal guilt that I was doing something wrong. This often made me feel that I was a bad person, further damaging my already fractured self-esteem.

I had a huge guilt complex as a result. This guilt complex caused me to maintain loyalty in situations where it was undeserved. I was not assertive and became a people pleaser to assuage my overwhelming sense of guilt. I had a terrible time deciding on what major to declare in college because I did not want to be disloyal to the professors and hurt their feelings. I couldn't even change hairdressers without feeling guilty! This sense of guilt and disloyalty is a terrible legacy to give children of divorce. It took several years of therapy for me to repair my fractured sense of loyalty.

Tom's Story

We had a very intact, close-knit extended family until the day mom and dad divorced. As a child, I remember being with aunts and uncles and cousins numerous times a year at my grandparents' home. They lived on a farm and we had great fun together, taking part in all the adventures that country life offered. These were great bonding times and I remember feeling very close and connected to my dad's family. Several of my male cousins were in essence brothers to me. That comradery ended the day mom and dad separated.

Because of my enmeshment with my mother, I felt that I had to choose between her family and dad's. In order to be loyal to mom, I felt that I had to distance from dad and his family. While I perceived this as a kind of loyalty and faithfulness to my mother, I felt tremendous guilt and some despair about cutting off from my extended family on my father's side.

This feeling was especially acute in my relationship with my grandmother, whom I believed dearly loved me. Research has indicated that many times when parents divorce, children feel the sting of rejection too. This was particularly true for me as it related to dad's family. It was as if I had not only rejected them in aligning myself with my mother but that they had also rejected me in siding with my dad. In essence, I struggled with both feelings of guilt about my emotional cut off with them and feelings of resentment at their rejection of me.

Consequently, when it came to family, I felt either anger or guilt most of the time. I began to realize over time that I was actually projecting that anger and guilt onto Bev and that I needed to resolve it. I remember feeling very hurt if Bev would have to do a paper for graduate school and could not spend time with me. I actually interpreted this as rejection. I would react to her with hurt and anger. I also remember feeling a need to distance from her to protect myself. I had learned to do this with my dad and his family. Needless to say, we were creating quite an interactive mess with our loyalty issues.

With the help of a compassionate and objective therapist, and through many painful conversations with my wife, I began the process of owning and resolving my guilt. Pursuing a second master's degree in counseling and many hours of prayerful meditation and Scripture reading also helped in this process of healing. I worked through the feelings of disloyalty relating to choosing mom's family. I began to be able to forgive dad, and pardon his family for choosing to support him. The anger and the guilt began to be resolved, as I forgave both them and myself for our reactivity to the wounds of divorce.

Not all parents play the guilt card as much as our parents did. But it would behoove parents who are divorced to pay close attention to how they respond when their children want to spend time with their ex-spouse or their ex-spouse's family. Any shadow of guilt inducement can create problems for them, even into adulthood. If ACODPs want to get to know estranged parents or family members, they should have the emotional freedom to make this choice, even if there are unpleasant consequences. They are adults and should have the liberty to decide for themselves, without a horrible sense of compunction and blame. What we would have given for the gift of this liberty.

Divorce Weakens Religious Life

Research illustrates that divorce also damages the religious life of a family. Families that went to their church, parishes, or synagogues regularly tend to abandon this practice after divorce. Further studies show that a healthy religious life is linked to certain benefits, such as better health and happiness and stronger values. The absence of these benefits can have negative effects on your social structure and on society as a whole. The loss of faith is not the only problem for ACODPs. The divorce can also have a negative affect on how they perceive religion, and on how they view God in general.

Elizabeth Marquardt in her article entitled "Children of Divorce: Stories of Exile" in *The Christian Century Magazine* points out that as many as half of today's twenty to thirty year olds have experienced the divorce of their parents. She says that, "This entire generation of young adults had been deeply affected by living in a society in which the possibility of lasting commitment is viewed with suspicion, and sometimes despair. Yet our culture and our churches have asked relatively few questions about the experience of children of divorce. We have failed to recognize that their parents' divorce shapes the spiritual journeys of people throughout their lives."

Marquardt shares that certain passages of Scripture, such as the story of the prodigal son, have little resonance for ACODPs. The son in the story rejected his family. ACODPs feel like they have no real family to reject. One person said, "There wasn't a stable enough family to go away from and come back to." Another evangelical Christian told Marquardt that he saw his father in the role of the prodigal son, leaving his family to seek his own fortune elsewhere. This man saw himself in the role of the father, waiting at the doorway for his loved one to return.

The fourth commandment to honor your father and mother presents problems for some ACODPs. A Roman Catholic told Marquardt the he had a hard time with the idea of honoring his parents. His questions were "Did they honor me? Did they even ask me before they decided to divorce?" Another man said, "My father does not deserve to be honored. He didn't think about the people who relied on him. He made a commitment to a spouse. He had a child. And then he didn't find a way to honor his commitments to them."

Marquardt challenges churches and parishes to find ways to minister to the special needs of ACODPs. They need to see that ACODPs can feel isolated and alone as a result of the grief and loss they experienced from their parents' divorces. It is especially important, she says, to welcome them into the church. We have found that often ACODPs can have the wrong idea of God because it is based on their notion of their parents. Their faith is challenged because they have lost hope in God and life, because of the pain and loss they have suffered from their parents' divorces. This can be very damaging to them, as well as thwarting to their religious life.

Bev's Story

My parents' divorce had both negative and positive effects on my religious life. My grief and loss caused me to look for a place to belong. There was a sweet group of elderly ladies who worshiped in a little church on the corner in my neighborhood. They sought out my siblings and I. They brought us food and treats. Often, they would bring us candy as they did their home visits. I started going to that church because I was so hungry for attention and love. It was one of the best things that I ever did in my life.

The negative aspect of my religious life was that as a result of my parent's divorce, I had a warped view of God. I viewed him similarly to how I saw my parents. God was the supreme authority, a kind of "Big G" in the sky, who did what he wanted with his children and said it was for their own good. So often my parents would make selfish choices and then rationalize them by saying that they were beneficial for me and that I would grow from them. My mom would beat me and punish me severely for simple offenses and I learned to fear making a mistake around her. I tried to be as perfect as possible to avert her wrath. This is what I did in my spiritual relationship with God as well.

The church I attended had very strict fundamental beliefs. They tended to view God as more judging and punishing than loving and caring. This fit in perfectly with the paradigm that I was in with my family. I was afraid of God in much the same way as I feared my mother. This made me feel that I had to earn my place with God. I thought I had to perform for God in order for him to love me. Like many of the subjects in Elizabeth Marquardt's article, I had a hard time grasping an unconditionally loving father. It took years of study, prayer, meditation, and searching the Scriptures for me to begin to grasp the idea that God unconditionally loved me.

One particularly inspiring moment in my spiritual life was watching the motion picture *The Hiding Place* as a young teenager. This movie was the story of Corrie Ten Boom, a Dutch woman, who helped the Jews hide from the Nazis in

World War II. Corrie and her family were arrested and placed in Auschwitz, a vile concentration camp. The movie is about her struggles there. My siblings and me could relate so well to Corrie and her sister, Betsy, as they suffered at the cruel, torturous hands of the Nazis. We had often felt like those innocent people, being punished for no good reason. The only difference between my siblings and me and the people of Auschwitz was that their enemy was very clearly defined. Our cruel, unreasonable enemy was our very own mother. My brother and sister and I still refer to our sibling gatherings as Auschwitz reunions because we actually feel like concentration camp survivors.

The part of Corrie Ten Boom's story that stood out to me was her struggle with why God allowed such horrible things to happen to such innocent people. I had that struggle in my own life and in my own family. I was not alone in my questioning. ACODPs often ask, "Why me?" or "Why my family?" Corrie found her answers in Scripture. Apparently, she had slipped a Bible into the camp and would read it to her fellow prisoners. She felt that she had a revelation when she read about the suffering of the apostle Paul in the book of Romans. Paul had been shipwrecked, stoned, falsely imprisoned, and left for dead and yet he wrote these words in Romans 8:38–39, "For I am convinced that nothing can separate us from the love of God. Death can't, and life can't. The angels won't and all of the powers of hell itself cannot keep God's love away" (TLB). This passage, along with Corrie's faith, inspired me to see that God did indeed love me unconditionally and, unlike my parents, did want the best for me. The courage of heroes like the apostle Paul and Corrie Ten Boom encouraged me to forge ahead in my life. This was very healing for my spiritual and emotional life, but many adult children of divorced parents have trouble seeing this.

It takes the sensitivity of religious leaders to be able to reach ACODPs because of their special needs. Churches and religious groups need to work hard to understand the particular struggles of adult children of divorced parents in order to teach, counsel, and comfort them.

Ministering to the vast emotional array of responses that ACODPs possess will help strengthen their religious life, as well as grow churches and parishes, which will benefit our communities.

Divorce Wounds Society As a Whole

In this chapter, we have seen that divorce takes its toll on society at large. It leaves couples bereft of parental mentors. It severs relationships with families and friends. It kicks the support out from under children. Divorce festers emotional cutoff that leads to divorces in the next generation. The loyalty issues that ensue from divorce plague children even as adults. These issues can create a problem for our entire culture.

How will ACODPs deal with their loyalty issues in providing care for their aging parents? Who will care for the fathers and mothers of divorce as they begin to age? As families are broken apart, who will be responsible for the care of their elders? Many adult children do not even know their aging relatives, much less have the ability and motivation to care for them when they are elderly. These questions create quite a problem for today's society, which must be dealt with and resolved.

Coincidentally, as we were writing this chapter, a good family friend of ours passed away. This man was a very giving community servant and was revered by many. He was also divorced. When he remarried, he took on the fathering of his widowed wife's four children. He was a wonderful father to them, but the attention he paid to his new family estranged his own children. This often happens when there is a divorce. The sad thing about his wake service the night before his burial was that although people from the entire community came to pay their respects, there were two people who were noticeably absent, his two oldest sons. It seems that the pain of their severed relationship was too great for them to bear. How tragic. Divorce indeed causes wounds to the social structure of individuals and to society. Healing these wounds is a huge challenge for this generation.

Chapter 9

Healing through Problem Solving

In the last chapter we saw how the lack of adequate role models can negatively affect adult children of divorced parents. One of the things in marriages that causes problems for ACODPs is their lack of healthy examples of problem solving and conflict resolution. It is common for conflicts to be resolved in painful and unhealthy ways in divorced families. The metaphor of being a dancer without ever having seen a dance certainly applies here.

Conflict resolution doesn't come as easy for ACODPs as it does for adult children from intact families. One of the biggest challenges in helping ACODPs with this process is to enable them to access memories of childhood and gain insight into how those memories affect their relationship today. The Digging Deeper Exercise in Chapter 7 is a good tool for them to use in doing this. ACODPs then need to develop understanding for each other, build empathy for themselves and each other, and promote connection in their marriage. The ingredients of awareness, understanding, empathy, and connection are keys for healthy problem solving among all couples, but are especially important for ACODPs who may not have seen them displayed in their families-of-origin. Problem solving in marriage is a skill worth learning. It can be hard work, but well worth the effort. This chapter is dedicated to helping ACODPs learn how to do this.

Solving problems in a healthy way was such a struggle for Tom and I early in our marriage. I would avoid conflict and try to be a pleaser and Tom would get angry and shut down. This was so frustrating for us. One of the things we learned that really helped us was learning how projection plays such a key part in our perceptions. We have learned in Chapter 7 that we project things onto our partner that we possess within ourselves and often don't want to see. By projecting these parts of ourselves onto our partner we can avoid having to face them within ourselves.

Relationship theorists say that 80 percent of all communication is projection. This means that what you accuse your partner of may be something you are actually guilty of, and what your partner criticizes in you has a certain element of truth as well. We learned early in our marriage that the best thing to do with criticism and projection was to embrace it and understand it, not to try so hard to defend against it.

Criticism and Projection

Studies show that criticism is one of the main causes for divorce in marital interaction. Criticism causes a negative cascading cycle between husband and wife that is very destructive. Much research has been done on the harmful aspects of this negative cascading cycle. Researchers have found that it usually follows a predictable path. One party criticizes; the other defends his or her position. The other partner then counters the defense, an argument ensues, and then both spouses shut down. This shutting down, or stonewalling, as it has been labeled, can be done verbally by saying things such as, "Leave me alone," or "We are not going to talk about this any more," or nonverbally by refusing to talk, walking out of the room, or, in extreme cases, leaving the premises. When both parties stonewall each other, the conflict does not get resolved. As these conflicts go unattended, there are layers of resentment that build up. These layers fester into the state of contempt.

Dr. John Gottman, one of the primary researchers of this negative cascading cycle in marital interaction, defines contempt as disdain or disrespect. Gottman says that couples that have contempt for each other no longer feel that there are problems with each other's behavior. They feel like the problem exists with each other's character. And they believe that character defects cannot be repaired. When couples are in a state of contempt, they usually feel hopeless and contemplate divorce.

In order for couples to stop this negative cascading cycle, they need to find ways to intervene before the cycle deteriorates. One way to do this is to help couples examine the criticism that has been made about them. If they can scrutinize their partner's criticism and see the element of truth in the projection, they will not be so defensive. Likewise, if they examine their criticisms, to see if they bear some of the qualities that they scorn within their spouse, they may be less likely to be so critical and negative in the first place. Separating truth from projection, when you are criticizing and when you are criticized, is helpful for both parties when trying to resolve marital conflicts.

Fair Fighting Rules

Seeing the truth in our projection was not the only helpful discovery we made in all of our searching to find healthy ways to resolve marital conflict. We have also picked up a few fair fighting rules over the last twenty-five years that will be beneficial for all couples, but especially for ACODPs who have fewer role models for this. One of the basic premises of fair fighting rules is that there will be marital fights. Many ACODPs avoid arguments and try to keep the peace at any price because they fear that they will suffer the same fate that their parents did. In order to fight fairly, ACODPs have to accept that fighting is inevitable. It is how you fight that is important. Just having rules to go by in conflict will help ACODPs be less fearful of conflict. These rules certainly helped us. The rules can be grouped into several categories. The first category is *how* to argue, the second is *when* to argue, and the third is *where* to argue.

How to Argue

- Approach conflict with a problem-solving attitude, not a position of being a victim, having to be right, or getting even.
- Don't say things that are so critical or attacking that there is no recourse for your spouse but to retaliate or leave. Remember, the goal is problem solving.
- Don't make threats during the argument. People say things that they regret in conflict. This can be difficult to take back and does tremendous damage.
- No blanket judgments or labeling is allowed. This means no name calling, tissue damage, property damage, or soul damage.

- Talk about the feelings underneath your anger, not just your anger. Instead of saying "You make me so mad," say, "When you do this, I feel this." Use The GIFT Exercise to help you.
- Stay on the topic. Don't throw in the kitchen sink. Focus on specific behaviors rather than character. Character assassinations breed contempt, and contempt leads to divorce.
- Stay at the same eye level. Look at each other when you are trying to resolve a conflict. It is harder to say hurtful, retaliatory things when you are looking your partner in the eye.
- Never use "never" or "always." Overgeneralizations are a true indication that you are being reactive about something.

When to Argue

- Don't argue after ten o'clock at night. You are much too tired to think rationally late at night.
- Don't leave in the middle of an argument without telling your spouse that you are doing so. Plan a time to come back and resolve your conflict.
- If you need time to cool down, collect your thoughts, or write down what is bothering you; do this at a mutually agreed upon time. Communicate to let your partner know what you need. Be considerate.

Where to Argue

- Don't argue in the dark. You can say things in the dark that you would not say in the daylight.
- Don't argue in the bedroom. This stigmatizes the place where you make love.
- Don't argue in public. Either you or your partner will be inhibited or embarrassed. This is not fair to both of you and hinders problem solving and conflict resolution.
- Do argue outside where you feel the wind and the earth. Getting in touch with the yen of life helps you think in a more problem-solving fashion. We had friends who were from China and they would only argue in their garden. It was amazing how helpful this was for them.

The Problem with Assumptions

Another fair fighting rule for couples that we found to be very helpful was to never assume your partner's behavior. Earlier, you learned that one big problem in marriage is reactivity. When childhood soul wounds are triggered, reactivity occurs. So often when ACODPs become reactive, they are dealing with the wounds they have around their parents' divorces. Viewing their marriage through this filter can cause them to see things in a skewed manner.

Bev had a real problem with this when we had marital conflicts. Whenever I was mad at her, she would immediately fear that I was going to leave. Her reactivity caused her to make up her own reality about me. She then assumed what I was thinking, feeling, and doing. These assumptions were not only false but they were destructive for our marriage.

There were many times early in our marriage when Bev would be really upset with me for something. I had no clue what was troubling her. She would create this whole scenario, complete with assumptions about me, that I had no part of. She would then accuse me of these perceived, assumed injustices and I would get angry and defend myself. I felt powerless trying to defend myself against something that was an error in the first place.

There is one illustrative example of unhealthy assumptions that stands out in our minds. We had been married about six months and I was working at a college as an administrator. Bev was working as a social worker and going to graduate school. Needless to say, her plate was pretty full. One of my fun jobs at the college was to be the announcer at basketball games. One particular weekend, the team had a tournament. They were to play Friday night, and all day Saturday. I was excited about calling these games. The tournament schedule was so rigorous and Bev was so buried with graduate school that I did not even think that she would want to attend.

I went about my business, planning meetings and setting up the agenda for the tournament, all the while not knowing that Bev was really hurt because I had not invited her or even included her in the planning. She assumed that I did not want to include her. She assumed that I did not have fun with her. Before the weekend was over, she had assumed that I was bored with her and did not want to be with her anymore! These assumptions couldn't be further from the truth. It took a while for me to get her to talk about what was bothering her. When she finally told me her assumptions, I was dumbfounded. "How could you assume such things?" I questioned. "They seemed like the right conclusions to draw from your behavior," was her reply. Her assumptions were totally false and based on her skewed perspective as an ACODP. After a very long and difficult discussion, we both concluded that we would always check out our assumptions. If we were presumptuous about each other's behavior, we would check it out. We committed to each other that in the future, in lieu of assuming, we would ask. It was one of the smartest moves we have ever made as a couple.

Behavior Change, Not Character Assassinations

Focusing on behavior rather than on character not only prevents divorce but it really helps couples resolve conflict in a more productive manner. So often couples move to character assaults because they are deeply hurt about the fact that they are not getting their needs met in the relationship. When you attack your partner's character, he or she has little recourse. It creates a great deal of hurt and defensiveness. When you challenge your partner's behavior, he or she has the option of change.

Discussing behavior instead of character also prevents contempt from creeping in and decaying a marriage. The best way to get your partner to change his or her behavior is to ask. You make think that this is basic information, but many adult children of divorced parents do not ask very well for what they want.

Adult children of divorced parents had requests when they were children. They had things that they wanted their parents to do. One of those things might have been to stop fighting, one may have been to act more loving, and one may have even been to stay together. Their parents did not listen to or honor their requests. As a result, ACODPs learned not to ask. This is exactly what Bev and I did.

The Story of Us

I had a hard time asking for what I wanted from Tom in our
relationship. I felt guilty saying that I wanted something.
I actually remember wanting him to read my mind, to make it
easier for me. Since he wasn't a psychic, he was not very
good at this. Often we would get into conflict because I was
so hurt that he would not know what I wanted. He felt guilty
that he couldn't meet my needs and frustrated with me
because I wouldn't ask. It took a long time for me to learn
how to actually ask for what I needed from Tom, without feeling guilty. I was surprised that once he knew what I wanted,
he actually wanted to meet my needs. This wasn't so easy for
me because of my suspicion.

Suspicion

Perhaps one of the greatest hurdles for ACODPs to overcome is the
feeling of suspicion when their partner changes. All couples can have
some degree of suspicion when their partner changes their behavior,
but for ACODPs it can be debilitating. Many adult children of divorced
parents like Tom and I have watched as their parents broke up and then
got back together, only to break up again. This created a great deal of
suspicion within us that the behavior changes they were making were
not sincere or real.

Because of watching their parents' unsuccessful methods of behavior
change, many adult children of divorced parents feel that the changes
their partner makes are superficial or contrived. Because of their parents' divorces, they feel dubious and distrustful of lasting relationships
in general. When they are brave enough to request change in behavior,
their suspicions are really peaked.

Early in our marriage, I had a real problem with this. I often doubted
Tom's sincerity when he would change his behavior. I lived by the
ridiculous romantic fantasy that if someone really loves you, they can
read your mind. Therefore, they will know your need without you ever
having to ask. I had such romantic, idealistic thoughts as: "If I have to
spell out change, it is not from the heart." "If I had to make the request,

then the behavior change wasn't sincere." "If he really loved me, he would just know what I wanted him to do." While these notions would make for a great romantic movie, they are unrealistic and unhealthy. Before you fault me for them however, take a look at where these idealistic beliefs came from.

Brain Chemicals and Love

When a person falls in love, his or her brain is flooded with chemicals. These chemicals include norepinephrine, dopamine, and phenylethylamine. These substances work together to make a kind of love elixir. They function in the brain much like an amphetamine, or its more common name, speed. So basically when you fall in love, you are on speed. Like amphetamines, you have a supernatural feeling when the drugs are working. You feel like you are invincible, like you can do almost anything. It makes the grass seem greener, the sky appears bluer, and life just seems better. However, those feelings are not real. The presence of these amphetamines actually creates an altered state of consciousness in a person. This altered state creates problems for the relationship.

Many times phenylethylamine can be referred to as the "bonding chemical" because it helps you to bond and really connect with your mate. It enables you to be totally tuned in to your partner. You hang on his or her every word. You finish his or her sentences. When you first fall in love, you automatically anticipate each other's needs. You do things for each other, special things, without ever even requesting them. You and your partner do all of this for each other without either of you having to ask. All of these behaviors lead you to the extremely misleading conclusion that you and your partner can read each other's minds. This erroneous conclusion is one of the reasons you love each other so much. Getting your needs met, without even asking, is a wonderful blessing, especially if you grew up in a home where there was divorce and you learned not to ask for what you wanted. The problem with these great feelings of bonding and closeness is that they are artificially, chemically induced by phenylethylamine and will not last.

Bev and I had a great deal of phenylethylamine when we first met. The brain chemicals were flowing madly when we fell in love. We finished each other's sentences and seemed to know what each other was thinking. Unfortunately, it caused us to draw the false conclusion or delusion that we were telepathic and could read each other's minds. The bad thing about this is that we started to expect it.

When we were dating, Bev would anticipate my needs. If I rubbed my head like I had a headache, she would go get two aspirin and a glass of water and bring them to me, without me even asking! As time went on, when I had a headache, I would start to wonder, "When is she going to bring me those aspirin?" I could have waited all day for her psychic powers to unfurl. Regrettably, I waited in vain. I wish, at that time, we were smart enough to know that what we were feeling was more brain chemicals than true telepathic ability, but we did not.

To further complicate the matter, we made up our own reality about why we did not meet each other's needs. We started thinking that we actually knew each other's needs, but did not want to meet them any more. We assigned false motives to each other such as: "She tricked me when we first met by being so caring. Now that she has caught me, she is not going to put out any effort." "He knows my needs and used to want to meet them. Now he doesn't care." "She is selfish and only does things for herself."

None of these were completely true. They were steeped in the delusion that our mate knew our needs and simply refused to meet them. This can cause ACODPs to feel betrayed. This replicates the same betrayal they felt in their families-of-origin when their parents divorced. You can see how this can cause problems for adult children of divorce. It caused its share of problems for Bev and I.

Like any other chemical that courses through the nervous system, the body builds up a tolerance to these natural amphetamines. After a while, the body simply can't manufacture enough phenylethylamine to produce love's special magic. As it declines in the system, the wonderful mind-reading capability, and the ability to anticipate each other's needs, diminishes with it.

It really helped our marriage to see this truth. That truth is that most people are not telepathic or psychic. They may get lucky with the help of certain brain chemicals early in the marriage, but as these chemicals fade, they resume their mortal qualities and they truly cannot read each other's minds. Not only do they not have telepathic ability but they also are not purposefully withholding love and care from their partner when they do not read his or her mind later in the marriage.

Fortunately, Bev and I learned that the unrealistic mind-reading fantasy, along with the negative illusion of betrayal, could be peacefully put to rest if couples would just remember this premise: It has been substantiated through research that, in relationships, your needs get met in proportion to your asking. In other words, you have a better likelihood of getting what you want in a relationship if you ask for it and do not expect your mate to "just know." We learned in the example of the elderly couple in the previous chapter that eventually couples can anticipate each other's needs, but it takes years for this to happen. In the meantime, Bev and I have learned to simply ask.

Anxiety and Healing

Often when ACODPs begin to do well in their marriage, they feel uncomfortable, even anxious. This was very true for our relationship as well. The fear of doom, along with watching our parents' repeated, unsuccessful attempts to reunite, caused us to become anxious when behavior change occurred. One of the things that helped us understand what was happening to us was studying Sigmund Freud's wish fulfillment theory in graduate school.

Freud hypothesized that with the fulfillment of every wish, there comes the fear that it will not be granted again. As a result, getting what you wish for causes anxiety. Getting what you long for creates a discomfort that it might not last. We say, "Getting what you want scares you to death." This fear might even cause people to sabotage their success, like lottery winners who win millions of dollars and end up penniless within a short period of time. They are just too anxious and uncomfortable with their prosperity and success.

This is especially true with adult children of divorced parents. They watched as their parents reunited and felt elated and excited about the future, only to experience terrible sadness when their parents eventually failed. This repeated disappointment really tormented us in our families. Both of us watched our parents split and come back together numerous times. While we were grateful for their efforts, it left us with the feeling that if we get our needs met, if we get what we wish for, it will not be granted again. Consequently, when we would reach a successful place in our marriage, we had tremendous anxiety that we were going to fall off of the proverbial hill that we had just conquered. This anxiety often caused us to sabotage our successes in much the same way Freud observed his patients doing.

In family therapy we have a saying that the person who wants the system to change the most is the one who will resist it the most. This resistance is unconscious, but it is still frustrating for couples. This unconscious resistance comes from the high levels of discomfort and anxiety that accompanies behavior change in a marriage. Unconsciously, couples try to get the system back to its previous homeostatic balance so that they do not have to fear that they will fail. Here is an example of how this worked in our marriage.

The Story of Us

Tom and I were in a class actually learning about Freud's wish fulfillment theory. Several days before the class, we had a discussion about Tom being preoccupied with graduate school. I was complaining to him that he had not been very affectionate lately. I am a touchy person and I like a lot of affection. I was making the request that he pay more attention to me and touch me more. (I am sure, by now, that you are not surprised that I would be the one whining and pursuing early in our marriage!) He agreed to be more affectionate with only a minimal amount of defensiveness. (See, we were learning.) As we were sitting in class, I was intently listening to the lecture. I barely noticed that he put his hand on my back and was gently stroking it.

What happened next was straight out of the annals of Freud's study. I started wincing and shrugging my shoulders, as if I was uncomfortable. I then stiffened up and became rigid and tight. I was completely unaware of what I was doing. This resistance to what I had wished for was completely unconscious to me. At that point, Tom leaned over and asked me what was wrong. I gave him a puzzled look and asked, "What are you talking about?" "You are so stiff and rigid. I thought you wanted me to be more affectionate. Don't you like it?" he questioned. At that moment, I had a revelation. Of course, it helped that we were in the very class that was teaching about what I was actually doing, but I realized that getting what I wanted was unconsciously making me feel very uncomfortable. My discomfort and anxiety was causing me to resist what I wanted the most. I was actually sabotaging my own marital success and standing in the way of getting what I wanted.

After class, we had a long talk about what had just happened that day. We both got a vivid illustration of how couples can thwart their own successes, if they are not more consciously aware of their behavior. We committed to ourselves and to each other that from that point on, when we requested a behavior change in our marriage, we were going to pay close attention to our own unconscious resistance. We were not going to let getting what we wanted scare us to death.

Lasting Behavior Change

There is one more concept that we want to share with you as adult children of divorced parents that really helped us in the area of conflict resolution and changing unhealthy behaviors. This is the concept about how change occurs in families and how it stands the test of time. We saw earlier that ACODPs have a high level of suspicion about their partner's motives for behavior change. They often doubt their mate's sincerity in changing. If they get over this hurdle, they have a tendency to be dubious that their partner's positive behavior changes will not last. Once again, many of these doubts occur as a result of watching their parents try to change their harmful behaviors and that these changes did not last the test of time. Their parents' marriages eventually failed. Their suspicion causes them to be much too critical of the durability and lasting effect of their spouse's change.

ACODPs even resist the idea of intentionality or "faking it till you make it" because they don't like the idea of change being fake or phony. Our theory is that they may have watched as their parents made feeble, phony attempts to convince each other that they had changed, so that they could reunite. ACODPs watch this charade as children and want no part of it in their marriage. This is exactly what we felt in our marriage. We both were suspicious and believed that if change was not sincerely heartfelt, then it did not count. One of the things we learned about change was very helpful in healing our suspicions.

In family therapy, we learned that there are two kinds of change that occur in family systems. One is called "first order change" and the other is called "second order change." First order change is behavioral and second order change is attitudinal. First order or behavioral change actually involves changing or reconstructing your behavior to reach a specific goal. This kind of change answers the following questions: "Are you acting differently?" or "Is your behavior different?"

Second order change, however, is a change of attitude. The operative question here is, "Do you feel differently?" This implies a change of the heart. Your behavior is different because you want it to be, because your heart directs or dictates that it changes. With second order change, you actually want to be different. This behavior change is an outgrowth of a change in your emotions and beliefs. When second order change occurs, you no longer have to practice intentionality. Your "want to" comes naturally. It takes practice and repetition for these changes to occur. This is where ACODPs have to give up their suspicion and doubt, and learn to trust the process.

Giving up our suspicion and doubt was difficult for us in resolving our conflicts. We both had a strong tendency to think that our partner's intentionality was fake and contrived. Our dubious nature as ACODPs caused us not to give each other credit for trying, and not to believe that the changes were real. We have since learned that if a couple practices first order change long enough, that is, changing their behavior, then second order change is more likely to occur. In other words, if a couple changes their behavior as an act of their will, the feelings will follow. If they practice first order change, eventually a second order or genuine heart change can occur. This did wonders for our marriage in helping us resolve conflict and learn to trust each other.

Chapter 10

Healing through Forgiveness

Webster defines forgiveness as the act of granting pardon to an offender or to cease to feel resentment against. Wow! What a tall order. For many of us adult children of divorced parents, and we include ourselves in this group, the act of granting pardon or ceasing to feel resentment can be very difficult. Forgiveness is one of the hardest concepts to grasp in relationships, yet there has been a plethora of research and material written on the value of forgiveness in marriage. Research is even showing that the ability to forgive is one of the main ingredients in healthy families.

ACODPs have to tackle the difficult concept of forgiveness from many angles. First, they have to learn to forgive their parents for the divorce and the painful things that led up to it. This can be easy for some, but feel impossible for others. Then, they have to forgive their spouse for the offenses he or she commits in the marriage. The challenge here is that their spouse can re-injure them in much the same way their parents did, thus making their spouse's offenses doubly hard to pardon. Finally, they have to forgive themselves for their shortcomings, and you know after reading the last few chapters that ACODPs bring a lot of baggage into marriage that can cause marital dysfunction. Like all adult children of divorced parents, we had our struggles with forgiveness. We would like to share a little of our journey with you.

Bev's Journey Toward Forgiveness

The story of my journey toward forgiveness is hard to tell. I am a very sensitive person, too sensitive in fact for my own good at times. I am easily moved to compassion and have a great deal of mercy. While this can be a gift, like all gifts it has its downside. Being so sensitive with others causes me to also be too sensitive myself. I can get my feelings hurt easily and can get taken advantage of. One of the greatest lessons that I have had to learn in life is to toughen up. I'm still learning it.

I have learned in working with all types of people that sensitive individuals have a harder time forgiving than others. Then, there are those people who can forgive with ease. How I envy them. A former minister of ours had the sanguine, vociferous salesman temperament. When he got upset, he would blow hard and cool down quickly. Once he let off some steam, he moved forward and didn't look back. He would forget the wrongs done to him and would seldom hold a grudge. While he tended to be somewhat insensitive at times, most sanguine people are, his temperament was appealing to me.

I, on the other hand, was not blessed with such a short memory of the wrongs that were done to me. I was easily and often aghast when people would do things that hurt me. I frequently thought, "How could they do that? I would never do such a thing." I thought that because I was sensitive, then everyone else should be as well. Most people in my life did not see things as I did, so consequently, I spent a lot of my life feeling hurt and mistreated. The regular atrocities that occurred in my childhood made it hard for me to contemplate forgiveness. It seemed that, most of the time, survival was the more necessary objective for my psyche. And I barely even did that.

There was such pain inside of me from my mother's verbal assaults and physical abuse, the violent fights between my parents, my brother's bout with drug and alcohol abuse, and the culmination of my father leaving and my parents' divorce, that I thought, "How could I forgive all of that? How could I move beyond it?" This whole idea of forgiveness was very tough for me to comprehend.

I shared with you previously that I started going to a neighborhood church when I was about ten years old. They taught me the evangelical doctrine of forgiveness in their very narrow, strict fundamental way. As with most of their dogma, they taught forgiveness as a duty, a command. While I personally believe that forgiveness is one of God's requirements and his forgiveness for our sins is the cornerstone of the Christian faith, I do not believe that God wanted a ten-year-old girl to feel so condemned because she had trouble forgiving her abusive, neglectful parents. But I did feel this condemnation, and in keeping with my "Miss Perfect" pleaser mentality, I did everything I could to oblige them.

The problem was that I tried so hard to forgive before I had a true understanding of what forgiveness was really all about. In order to comply with the request of my church leaders, I simply put the pain and hurt of my family out of my mind. I just chose not to think about it, all the while thinking that I was forgiving them. Basically what I was doing was repressing my pain and unforgiveness. Like all emotions that are repressed, they eventually emerge. They can come out emotionally by having problems with depression, anxiety, and other menacing mental maladies, or they can materialize physically with such psychosomatic disorders as migraine headaches, ulcers, insomnia, and worse. My repressed emotions surfaced both mentally and physically in my life.

I suffered from headaches, stomach problems, insomnia, anxiety, and eventually depression. I was not sure what was wrong with me. I thought that I was just sad because of the terrible circumstances that I was living in. While these severe conditions did not enhance my mental and physical state, my repressed anger and bitterness were debilitating me, and I did not even know it. Whenever I would get anxious or depressed, I would feel very guilty. I thought that I was a bad person and a faithless Christian, so I would push these feelings even further down into the recesses of my psyche. To further complicate my situation, I would compensate for feeling this despair by trying to talk myself into seeing the good in each situation. I would see the silver lining in the dark clouds of my life. Considering the good in bad circumstances can be very helpful unless you are repressing the bad to keep from feeling the pain. In psychoanalytic theory, the process of avoiding the bad and overemphasizing the good is called reaction formation. Basically, reaction formation is compensating in an opposite direction to avoid feeling a certain emotion or dealing with a certain reality.

Now, you might think that reaction formation and intentionality are the same thing, but they are not. Both of these concepts require that you act a certain way no matter how you feel, but with intentionality, you are completely aware of how you are feeling and you consciously choose to do the opposite. With reaction formation, you are not consciously aware of how you are feeling and you respond in a contrary manner in order to repress your true feelings. My reaction formation was very unhealthy for me emotionally and physically. I thought that I was following the Biblical mandate to forgive and all the while I was simply repressing my feelings, and my body was keeping score.

It wasn't until graduate school that a very wise professor suggested that some of my physical and emotional maladies might have their roots in repression and unforgiveness. "How could this be?" I thought. I believed that I had forgiven my parents. I assumed that my seeing the positive in all of the negative was proof of this. He suggested that maybe the work with my childhood pain and my parents' divorce was not finished, that perhaps I should explore my anger about them. "Explore my anger! I couldn't do that. Why, that's malicious, ugly, and down right un-Christian," I thought. I was pleased with myself for my sinless state of sympathy toward my perpetrators. If this sounds prideful, that's because it is. I have a hard time now believing that I could have been so deluded. But I actually thought that I was doing the right thing in repressing the pain of my parents' divorce and reframing it in such a positive way.

Since that time, I have learned a great deal about the difficult, yet amazing, process of forgiveness. I have learned what forgiveness is and what it is not. One of the things that I discovered is that, in order to forgive, you can't repress the offenses against you. If you do not see them as crimes, then you have nothing to forgive. This was a heavy concept for me to grasp. I thought that if I saw the offenses committed against me as damaging then that would in some way be unforgiving. To keep from doing this, I made up excuses for my offenders, particularly my parents. I minimized their crimes. I ignored the heartbreak that they caused me. These resolutions seemed positive to me, but they were actually standing in the way of my actually forgiving them.

One of the things that helped me to face my pain and see the damage that my parents caused me was learning what forgiveness actually is. My clouded perspective taught me that it was somehow suppressing feelings instead of expressing them. I learned that forgiveness is honest. It speaks the truth and holds nothing back. It does not repress or suppress the truth, but acknowledges it, feelings and all. That is what actually makes it forgiveness. If what you are pardoning is not true, then the pardon is false as well. Lewis Smedes in his classic book, *Forgive and Forget: Healing the Hurts We Don't Deserve*, says that, " Forgiveness is honest because it happens along with honest judgment, honest pain and honest hate. True forgivers don't pretend they don't suffer. They do not pretend that the wrong does not matter much." I could not be a true forgiver until I stopped pretending and became honest about my pain.

As I did this, another very complex and difficult aspect of forgiveness began to rear its ugly head. This was Dr. Smedes' concept of honest hate. When I first heard this, I could not believe my ears. "Did he say hate?" I wondered. I was sure he was mistaken. "Wasn't there a scriptural mandate against hating? Now theologians were saying that it was necessary. What was happening here?" I questioned. I will never forget the words of Smedes' manuscript as they jumped off the page at me. He penned, "None of us wants to admit that we hate someone. It makes us feel mean and malicious .... But we do hate people. Only an unearthly saint or an unfeeling oaf gets far in life without hating someone." He had caught me red-handed. His convicting script had found me guilty. I hated the people in my life and I had to admit it, confess it, and deal with it in the process of learning to forgive.

This was the hardest thing that I have ever done. Not only did I have to surrender my repression, which had become such a good saintly cover for me, but I also knew that I had to feel the pain that inspired my hatred. Once I started being honest, the pain came, and came, and came. With it, came the hate. Oh, how I hated the hate. I didn't like feeling rancor and resentment toward my parents. I did not like judging their actions. I did not like feeling that justice needed to be served on them. I wasn't merciful with their behavior and the outcome any more. I did not spend much time with them because it was so painful for me. Amidst all of this dislike and discomfort however, something remarkable happened. I began to feel a freedom, a cleansing, a choice to move in a healing direction. It was a choice to forgive, to truly forgive with integrity this time. This forgiveness was complete with all of the honest judgment and hate that forgiving with honor and truth has to offer the soul of the forgiver. With this forgiveness, came a freedom from the bondage that had enslaved me, and I was not even aware of it. I felt like a great weight had been lifted off of me. I felt a purging that was healing. I learned that forgiveness is a wonderful gift that you give yourself.

Along the way, I began to see my repression as resistance to really forgiving. When I became honest, I started asking questions about forgiveness. Since that time, many ACODPs have asked the same questions to me. We thought that it would be very helpful to address these questions with you.

What if the person who hurt me does not deserve to be forgiven?

As I began to feel the pain of my mother's abuse and my father's abandonment, I must have asked myself this question a million times. There were things that my parents did that I could not, and still cannot, comprehend. These things loom larger when I see how much I love my own children and want what is best for them. I cannot imagine doing to them some of the things which were done to me. Because of this, I struggled so much with whether they deserved forgiveness, and my constant conclusion was to the contrary.

I tried threatening myself with the biblical mandate to forgive. I regularly prayed the Lord's Prayer, specifically the part requesting that the Lord forgive my trespasses as I forgave those who trespassed against me. This was to no avail. I needed a way to answer this question that would satisfy me. I was determined not to repress or comply simply to please others again.

My search for answers to this question led me to several great awarenesses. The first is that forgiveness is exactly what its name says. It is *for giving*. It is a procedure *for giving* something which is not deserved. The paradox about forgiveness is that it is not only *for giving* to others, it is also *for giving* to ourselves. When I began the process of forgiving my parents, a part of me was healed. This act of forgiveness was curative for me. So, the first part of my answer to the above question is: Forgive those who have hurt you because it is good for you.

In a way, forgiveness can be a selfish act. We forgive others because we benefit. I have a friend who is a therapist. She tells her clients that, "Unforgiveness is like taking poison and waiting for someone else to die." In other words, you will be the one suffering by constantly wishing ill on your offender. Forgive because it heals you, not because it pardons the unpardonable in your life.

The second realization I had was far more altruistic than narcissistic. It is the example of the sinless Christ who walked this planet and suffered great, unfair persecution and abuse. He ultimately sacrificed his life as a symbol of his forgiveness for his children who were not sinless as he was. This idea was an inspiration for me to be more sacrificially forgiving of those who have caused me pain.

The last thing that helped me answer the question, "What if they don't deserve to be forgiven?" is the fact that I want forgiveness for the sins of omission and commission that I commit in relationships. It would be illogical, not to mention hypocritical, to ask for Tom and others to give me what I was not willing to give to them.

Does forgiveness mean that what the offender did was all right?

No indeed, forgiving is not excusing. Forgiving a person is an act of pardoning them *because* they are guilty, because what they did was not right, not because it was. To forgive someone means that you hold them responsible for what they have done, you put blame on them for their offense, and still the act itself is *for giving* them pardon. So, forgiveness in no way means lack of guilt, responsibility, or blame. Forgiveness means pardoning a person in spite of all of this. I tell ACODPs that forgiveness does not mean that what your perpetrators did was all right. It simply means that you are choosing to be all right, regardless.

Does forgiveness mean that the perpetrator should resume the same relationship with you that they had previously?

Not necessarily. Forgiveness is not simply toleration. If you forgive someone for their painful unhealthy actions, then you obviously want the behavior to stop. If you forgive your spouse for having an affair, this does not mean that they can continue their extramarital relationship. Forgiving an offense does not mean that you have to continue to endure it.

If I forgive someone, does that mean that I am automatically supposed to trust them?

Part of what holds ACODPs back from forgiving is that they fear that the harmful behaviors will continue and they will be hurt again. This was what happened often in their families-of-origin, and they fear that it will happen to them again. They cannot trust that the offender will stop his or her offensive behavior, therefore they do not want to forgive. Forgiveness and trust are two different things. Forgiveness is granting pardon for an offense. Trust is believing in a person's integrity and ability to change. Trust is a confidence that you were heard and that things will be different.

Some people mistakenly feel that since they have forgiven, they cannot mention the offenses committed against them ever again. This is not true forgiveness, nor is it completely healthy. When you forgive someone, the healthiest thing you can do is to talk about the future and the behavior changes that need to occur. We will teach you an exercise at the end of this chapter that helps couples walk through this process of forgiveness and building trust. You can forgive someone and still have to build trust. After forgiveness has occurred, trust does not come automatically or all at once. It has to be earned.

Does forgiveness mean forgetting?

No, you can forgive someone and still remember their offense. It's a good thing to remember, because if you repressed the transgressions like I did, then you would be setting yourself up to be wounded again and again. Remembering helps you set boundaries so that you can protect yourself. Bringing up the offense is not necessarily making the person pay or not forgiving. When an offense has occurred, you may have to bring it up from time to time to build trust or clarify behavior change. What is not healthy is to use these offenses against your partner or throw them back in the faces of the offender, as if to punish them, or never let them off the hook for hurting you. Clarifying behavior, setting boundaries, and building trust are good reasons for not forgetting. Bringing up offenses and using them against the offender, holding a grudge, or making the wrongdoer suffer is not.

Does forgiveness happen all at once?

We believe that forgiveness is a process, a commitment to start the precarious procedure of pardoning a perpetrator. Forgiveness is not an automatic act of the soul. It takes time. The greater the offense, the longer it can take. Some people can forgive more quickly than others. Some need a great deal of time and space to be able to forgive. If the wrongdoer continues the offensive behavior, then you have to forgive repeatedly. This can be difficult, but if you commit with all of your soul's energy to do this, then you are on the road to forgiving. It may still take some time to get there. Be patient with yourself. Forgiveness is a process, not an event.

How do you know that you have forgiven someone?

This one was really hard for me because I thought that I had forgiven when I had really just denied the pain of the offenses committed against me. When I finally did own these offenses, I was not sure how I would know if I had truly forgiven my offenders. At first, I had a strong desire for vengeance. The definition of vengeance is to seek revenge, to retaliate injury for injury, to somehow even the score. I felt these feelings. I wanted people to feel the pain that I felt. While this seemed fair to me, I knew that this could not be forgiveness.

I later changed my goal from vengeance to justice. The definition of justice is the quality of being just and equitable or the administering of deserved punishment. "Now that sounded more humane," I thought. "Perpetrators deserve to be punished for their wrongdoings," was my rationale. But soon I realized justice was not forgiveness because I was still wanting the offender to pay. I realized that forgiving is letting go of the desire for vengeance or justice. It is *for giving* pardon. You know you have forgiven someone when you can let go of the outcome of the situation, when you can be at peace with the burden you carry regarding the offense, when you can wish your perpetrator health. This is hard because some perpetrators do not deserve health. In order to achieve any kind of wellness, most offenders will have to face the ugly parts of themselves. I realized that even in this process there is an amazing element of justice. Regardless of what happens to the offender, the act of forgiveness is *for giving* them pardon and letting it go.

We see too often that ACODPs wound each other, and quickly ask for forgiveness. The person wanting forgiveness has little remorse, and the hurting person offers pardon out of guilt or duty, not from their heart and soul. In this situation, true forgiveness has not taken place. In order to truly forgive with integrity, both parties have to thoroughly consider the crime and give the process the emotional and moral energy it deserves. This frees the soul of the forgiver, as well as the forgiven, to move ahead unencumbered with the weight of the offense in their lives.

Requesting Forgiveness

We have spent some time and energy discussing the aspects of forgiveness for the forgiver, but there are some considerations and requirements for the offender that need to be mentioned as well. When an offender is requesting forgiveness, there are several things that they need to possess. The first is genuine sorrow for the wrongs they have done.

Genuine Sorrow

Sorrow is a regret or remorse for the offense they have committed. It really helps if the offender not only expresses sorrow but in that sorrow requests forgiveness. The simple statement, "Will you forgive me for the wrong I have done?" is humbling and leads to repentance.

Empathy

In addition to sorrow, the offender needs to have empathy for his or her victim. They need to feel what the offended person felt, put themselves in his or her place, and experience what it was like being in the shoes of the injured party. This empathy then causes the offender to feel contrition for his or her crime. Once sorrow and empathy are in place, then the offender needs to put the finishing touches on his or her request for forgiveness with repentance.

Repentance

To repent is an act of turning away. It is a turning around, a changing of your ways, because of the sorrow you feel for your crimes. Repentance connotes a desire to make things right, to atone, or to make amends. Repentance is the act of making reparation for wrongs done.

When an offender feels repentant, he or she no longer wants to do the hurtful behaviors that caused the problems in the relationship. This means that if the perpetrator is truly sorry, he or she will try not to commit the offense again.

A Tool for Forgiveness

Struggling so much with forgiveness in our own marriage and with other ACODPs, we knew that we needed a tool that would bring understanding, enhance mutual empathy, and foster forgiveness. A tool was needed to organize the forgiveness process in such a way that deeply wounded couples could participate in it more easily. We found that since ACODPs are more apt to suffer from such deep hurts as chemical dependency, alcoholism, neglect, abuse, and severe emotional problems, they needed extra help in being able to ask for and receive forgiveness in their marriages. The tool we developed is called The Forgiving Experience. Not only is it helpful for adult children of divorce but it has been useful for all of the couples we have treated. There are several foundational premises or building blocks of this exercise that would be helpful for you to learn.

Premises of The Forgiving Experience

The first premise we built on in the forgiveness process was derived from Alcoholics Anonymous. We replicated a form of their fourth and fifth steps, in which individuals are encouraged to do a moral inventory of the wrongs they have done and begin the process of making amends for them. In our tool, however, it is the offended party that makes a list of offenses that his or her partner has committed. The list includes the difficult affronts that the offended partner cannot seem to forgive. This is so that the offended partner can express the entirety and depth of their pain in an uninterrupted manner, and move the couple toward healing.

The second premise of The Forgiving Experience is based upon an exercise called the "container," which is a part of Hendrix's Imago Relationship Theory in his book, *Getting the Love You Want*. Hendrix uses this tool to enable couples to express anger and resentment toward each other in a safe and constructive environment. One partner shares his or her anger about past wounds and hurts and the other serves as a container for their rage. Rather than reacting or defending, the offender puts on his or her psychic armor, stays calm, and listens with empathy. This allows the offender to hear what the mate is saying without being defensive or reactive.

There are two main purposes for this part of the exercise. First, it allows for the offended partner to say what hurts him or her, and give the situation the anger and emotion it deserves. Second, it enables the emotion to once and for all be expressed and resolved, so partners can put the past behind, let the water flow under the proverbial bridge, and move ahead in the relationship, unencumbered by past pain.

While Hendrix's process allows couples to exorcise stored rage from their marriage, providing some symptomatic relief for their bitterness and resentment, it lacks the motivation to bring the couple to true forgiveness. Therefore, we added a spiritual component to the forgiveness process.

First, we encourage adult children of divorced parents to view themselves, their parents, and their partners as fellow sojourners in the rough sea of life, victimized by the pain of divorce and the failure of their family to stay afloat. For this reason, ACODPs can have mutual empathy for those whom they have hurt and for those who have hurt them. This empathy can move them toward forgiving their partner more easily. Second, we teach couples to use God's grace for man's sin as an inspiration to forgive each other. We encourage couples to forgive each other, in a response of gratitude to your awareness of the grace and mercy of God.

The last premise of The Forgiving Experience is based on the work of Lewis Smedes, which postulates that in order for true forgiveness to occur, and trust to be rebuilt, several things must happen. The person asking for forgiveness must truly feel the pain that he or she has inflicted upon the offended party. The partner requesting forgiveness needs to be willing to empathize with his or her victim and understand why he or she committed the offense, so that change can occur. This is not an easy task because it often brings up guilt that the perpetrator does not want to feel.

We have systematized these premises into an eight-step process, in order to simplify it for hurting couples. The eight steps of the Forgiving Experience follow.

THE FORGIVING EXPERIENCE: A TECHNIQUE FOR HEALING

Step 1: Make a list of offenses.

The offended partner makes a list of the main hurts and resentments in the marriage. The offended partner is as thorough as possible and lists these offenses with the goal of finally letting them go.

Step 2: Share the list of offenses with the offender.

The offended partner shares the list with the offender, along with the painful feelings that these hurts have caused. The offended spouse gives each action the anger it deserves without causing damage to tissue, property, or soul. The offended is instructed to share personal feelings, not attitudes or opinions. The "When you ..., I feel ..." dialogue is practiced here.

Step 3: The offender listens with empathy and compassion.

The offender feels the pain of the victim with compassion and empathy for the crimes he or she has committed. He or she puts him or herself in the offended partner's shoes and experiences what it was like for the victim to be hurt. The offender's job here is to listen with empathy, and not become defensive or reactive.

Step 4: The offender states empathy.

The offender makes an empathic statement about the pain he or she has caused. It is not just important to feel the pain he or she has inflicted on others; the offender must also make a statement to this effect. The statement might be something like, "I now realize how much pain I caused you by having an affair. It must have been so painful for you."

Step 5: The offender requests forgiveness.

The offender asks, "Will you please forgive me?" The request for forgiveness is essential for humility and repentance to occur.

Step 6: The offended starts the process of forgiveness.

The offended partner prayerfully commits to begin the process of forgiveness.

Step 7: The offender promises change.

The offender promises, with the intent of his or her heart and soul, to make changes in the future. With their repentance comes the willingness to change. Specific behavioral changes are mentioned. We have found that many of the barriers to forgiveness in marriage are due to the lack of trust that the offender's behavior will change in the future. This step insures that change is a part of the repentance or atonement process. It also aids in the building of trust between the partners.

Step 8: The offended shows gratitude.

The offended partner responds with gratitude and/or appreciation toward the offender for the sorrow and humility shown.

The Forgiving Experience is practical in that it leads couples through a logical process of forgiving that is both doable and resolvable, and at the same time, it is deeply healing for each person individually, and for the couple collectively. Some soul-murdering crimes can only be forgiven with God's grace. The eight steps of The Forgiving Experience may be the hardest eight steps that ACODPs can take. We have found that if couples will take them though, they can actually heal the bitterness and contempt that causes their marriages to atrophy and leads to divorce. The process of forgiveness helps adult children of divorced parents beat the odds against them in marriage, and is well worth incorporating as a ritual in marriage.

Chapter 11

Critics, Questions, and Comments

Since we committed to write this book and share our findings and our stories with audiences across the country, we have received a great deal of support. Some of the people who have supported us, identifying the specific symptoms of adult children of divorced parents, have given us permission to share parts of their stories with you. We will do this later in this chapter. First, we want to address the critics.

Dealing with Critics

Among the generous support we have received there have also been a few critics and naysayers. These opponents do not believe that divorce should be singled out as such a problem for children and adults. After all, they argue, some children of divorced parents come out relatively unharmed. Inevitably, the critics want the blame for the problems that ACODPs face to be placed somewhere else. Critics of Tom's story say that his problems could have come from emotional incest, not divorce. Opponents of Bev's story often say that her problems could have come from an abusive home. In sharing our stories and identifying the specific symptoms of ACODPs, we are not saying that being children of divorced parents is the only way we could have manifested these symptoms. With any set of specific characteristics, there can be a plethora of causes that contribute. We do, however, see that some specific problems we have experienced in our own marriage *are* a direct result of our parents' divorces. All we are trying to do is share these problems with other ACODPs who may have some of the same symptoms. This helps us all feel like we are not alone.

Our concern with these critics is that we feel that they are trying to make divorce seem better than is realistic. They are trying to minimize its effects on children and adults because they do not want to admit that we have an entire generation at risk due to the faulty thinking on the part of their parents and society at large. Society's prevalent notion that children can survive divorce unscathed is simply not true.

We live in a culture in which we hesitate to talk about the consequences of divorce for kids. In part, this is because there are sometimes necessary reasons for divorce such as abuse or violence, but in part, because we live in a divorce culture, in which "no fault" is the norm. Parents feel that they should not have to sacrifice their happiness for the sake of their children's emotional well being. This opinion has contributed to the current high divorce rate in our country.

Divorce is now an epidemic in our nation, and the sad thing is that many people are reporting that they are no happier having ended their marriages. This means that there is a large group of children who are wounded, and for what purpose? Continuing to try to blame our problems on other causes than divorce seems to be a way to avoid dealing with this cultural dilemma. Surely there can be other contributing causes for the troubles we have experienced, but that is no reason to ignore the obvious. Helping ACODPs to identify their symptoms and find a path of healing is working to help them beat the odds of divorce in their own marriages. Let's continue the trend.

We did not do empirical research to determine if all ACODPs have these characteristics to a statistically significant percentage; we have simply interviewed couples and observed our own clients. The feedback we have received from them and the changes that we saw in our own marriage showed us that we were on to something. We were becoming aware of something significant. Perhaps the greatest responses we have received were the "ah ha" reactions we heard as we shared this information with wounded ACODPs. The awareness and insight that there was a reason for their troubling behavior was very relieving for them. For some, it was merely eye opening; for others it was freeing; for many it was healing. It gave reason to their pain. It explained their pathology, and it provided for them a map of healing. This map has been well-traveled by two ACODPs who have stepped in the holes and tripped and fell down the hills where others are about to go. They are grateful to have a tour guide. It is our hope that this book can guide many others.

Miserable Marriages

When we speak about ACODPs, there is at least one person in every audience who is in a miserable marriage and says that being in this situation makes them grumpy, irritable, and unhappy. These people are worried because they tend to take out their frustrations on their children. They then think that their children are suffering because of their miserable marriage. Since this is the case, they feel that their only solution is dissolution of their marriage. These parents rationalize that divorce is a better option for their children, but current research is pointing out that children have another opinion.

According to a 15-year study conducted by University of Nebraska researcher Paul Amato, only 30 percent of children of divorce had improved outcomes. This leaves a whopping 70 percent that were actually worse off. Another longitudinal study of adolescents conducted by psychologist Rex Forehand at the University of Georgia had similar findings. He found that even though negative aspects of the marriage existed before the divorce, it was the divorce itself, and the accompanying disruption of the family, that was associated with adolescent adjustment difficulties. Similar studies conducted with a nationally representative sample of families have shown that the negative effects of divorce on children are greater and more consistent than those associated with marital discord. This suggests that the problems children have adjusting after the divorce are not simply a continuation of the predivorce marital friction. It is the trauma of the divorce itself that causes the greatest problems. Both Tom and I have personally experienced this.

Bev's Story

My parents were a high conflict couple. There was a great deal of destructive violence in my family. By all accounts, I should be the child that would fare better after the divorce. This was not the case, however. The divorce was the fatal blow that crushed an already fractured family. That blow was the final kick in the teeth for us kids. It seems that statistics are backing this up. Studies show that even when both parents are yelling, hitting, and slapping, kids do not make the connection between their parents' behavior and the breakup of the marriage. This connection is too abstract for them to grasp. The notion that if the parents are miserable, then the kids will be miserable is simply not so. Statistically, the misery comes for the kids after the divorce. It certainly did for me.

Now, you may wonder if we feel that people who are experiencing violence should stay in a violent marriage for the sake of the kids. We feel that violence in marriages should not go untreated. We will answer this question in more detail in the question section of this chapter.

Times Are Changing

Obviously our stories of our parents' divorces have some of the worse-case-scenario ingredients. In our parents' divorces, there was emotional cutoff, parents playing us as pawns against each other, loyalty issues laced with parental guilt that warped our sense of compunction and kept us from whole sides of our families, and severed relationships that could not seem to be restored. Not all children of divorce experience such devastating consequences.

Several critics have argued that the fact that our parents' divorces occurred in the sixties and seventies may have played a big part in the depressing pessimistic outcomes of our families. In those days, women were more dependent on men. They did not have careers of their own, their earning potential was much lower, and fathers were less apt to be involved in the lives of their children before and after the divorce. This meant that divorce would have more devastating effects on families like ours, not to mention the fact that there were fewer families divorcing during that time. As a result, we felt more isolated and alone.

Times have changed somewhat. Many women have their own careers so that their income may not suffer as much. Fathers are taking more responsibility for their children and spending more time with them. Organizations like The National Fatherhood Initiative, Smart Marriages, and Promise Keepers have been established to encourage fathers to become more a part of their children's lives. Several books have been written about divorce, and postdivorce resources are available for all family members. Maybe these factors could make divorce a little kinder to this generation than it was to ours. We are very glad for all of these resources, but our goal is still to prevent divorce as much as possible, so that children will be less at risk even in these kinder times.

As we present on adult children of divorce across the country, we have received many questions via e-mail and in person. We thought that it would be helpful for us to list some of the most frequently asked questions and our humble attempts to answer them.

Common Questions

Should unhappy couples stay together for the sake of the children?

Since we started researching this book many couples have come to us for marital counseling. Some were familiar with the research about children and divorce, and some were not. We felt a responsibility to share these findings with them. In almost every situation, the research showing the negative consequences for children of divorce motivated them to try harder to work on their marriage. Of particular interest to many of them was the information that the damage of divorce is a cumulative experience. Its impact increases over time and rises to a crescendo in adulthood, strongly affecting ACODPs' ability to have healthy marriages themselves. Most of the couples with whom we work desire to put in extra effort to save their dying marriages after learning this information.

There are some marriages in which divorce seems to be the only solution. But for couples who feel that they are in a drowning marriage, they need to throw their union a life preserver. They need to do whatever they can to prevent divorce from damaging their children. Some of you in loveless marriages may be resisting this statement, but working on your marriage has never been easier in this day and age, with all the resources and skills-training programs available to you. We utilize many of these skills and programs, including our own soul-healing love model, to put couples back on the road to happiness. We have seen many couples, who were sure that they were doomed, come into therapy as a last-ditch effort to try to save their children the heartache of divorce. Many have stayed together. A lot of couples have actually fallen in love again. Some have chosen to make the best of their situation for their children and have improved their relationship to a better point. A few have found ways to stay in their marriage and tolerate their situation for their children's sake. The few tolerant souls we have treated have become aware that they may not be any happier as single people, thus they would cause their children unnecessary suffering. We whole-heartedly believe that couples who are in low-conflict, lifeless marriages should do everything possible to breathe life into their marriage for their sake and for the sake of their children.

Should violent couples stay married for their kid's sake?

Violence is not an acceptable means of conflict resolution in families. The most common belief is that violent partners cannot change. Research shows that abusive partners are harder to treat and more likely to relapse. This difficulty has caused many to believe that divorce is the only solution for abusive marriages.

In recent years, there have been several marital and family programs that have been more successful in treating these abusive people and families. Our own soul-healing love model has been able to help abusive mates get in touch with the pain of their childhood abuse and teach them healthier alternatives to violence in solving their marital problems. Ours is not the only program that has successfully treated conjugal crime. The website we designed for ACODPs lists several programs that have successfully treated family violence.

To answer the above question clearly for you, if you or your children are in danger, it is unwise to stay in a perilous situation just to prevent divorce. Divorce may be the only option if your partner will not get help, if he or she thinks that abuse is a good solution to problem solving, if he or she will not stop the abusive behaviors, or if you and your children continue to be in imminent danger physically or psychologically.

If you are already divorced, how can you help your children deal with the trauma?

Most children will suffer from your divorce. It is a good idea to check your guilt at the door and just accept this fact. Kids need to be able to talk about how they feel, without feeling like this is unacceptable to you. Following are a few rules that will help you.

- Talk to your children about what is going on. When they reach adolescence, tell them why you divorced. Leave out the sordid details or character assassinations of your partner. Telling them about your mistakes eases their fears and makes them feel more hopeful.
- Remember that divorce is not something that was settled once. Children and adults have a recurring need for information and support through life's major developmental passages.
- Make sure you tell them regularly that the divorce was not their fault and that both parents still love them very much. Most children harbor a fear that they somehow caused the breakup.
- Don't trash or belittle your ex-spouse in front of your children.
- Think about the situation with your family systemically. In other words, think what is best for the family, not just for yourself.
- If getting even is your goal, do not use the children in this process. Don't play your kids as pawns against each other.
- Don't grill your kids about your ex-spouse.
- Visits for the noncustodial parent should be generous.
- Noncustodial parents should visit frequently and regularly, even if it is painful for the parent to always be saying good-bye. Just think about how hard it is for the children.
- Children should not be kept from noncustodial parents to make a point or get even. This only hurts the kids.
- Parents should work together on parenting issues as much as possible. This peaceful collaboration on the child's behalf is priceless to them. This can be a difficult task, but is truly in the children's best interest.
- Divorce creates a fragile bond with at least one, and often both, parents, for this reason you need to be vigilant in giving them consistent support as much as possible.
- Custody arrangements should consider the specific needs of the children and should change as the children change and grow. Custody arrangements for an eight-year-old may be very different from those of a fifteen-year-old.

- Immediately after the divorce, try to keep the children's lives as consistent as possible in terms of location, school, and extra-curricular activities. They have already had enough change for one lifetime.
- Keep your children connected to the extended family of the noncustodial parent. It will make life easier for them.
- Be sensitive to their guilt and loyalty issues. Don't make them choose sides. This is destructive for their souls.
- Read books, find resources, get therapy, and seek out support groups for your kids when needed. There are plenty of these out there to choose from.

How do you help your grown children deal with divorce?

The most common mistake parents of adult children make is to assume that because they are adults, the divorce will not be as traumatic for them. Parents often enroll their adult children in a friendship relationship and confide in them as to the sordid details of why the marriage failed. This usually causes the ACODP to feel like he or she has to take sides, creating a great many loyalty issues. Not only are they caught in the crossfire of the divorce but they have to hear their parents share defaming details about each other. This can be very difficult and damaging for them. You have seen in this manuscript that divorce has a cumulative effect on children, often reaching a pinnacle in adulthood. Be sensitive to this. Give your adult children the support they need during adulthood as they deal with the divorce.

As divorced parents, can you give us ways to help our ACODPs find the right mate?

Most parents of divorced children fear that their children will make the same mistakes that they did. They are aware that their children are wounded and somewhat handicapped in the areas of dating and mating. The best thing parents can do is to share their relationship mistakes with their children. Don't run them into the ground or act too fearful that your children will follow in your footsteps. Share your insights with your children about their romantic partners. Do this respectfully and explain your concerns. Try to be positive and encouraging of their relational skills. Let them know that you have confidence in their relationship abilities as much as possible.

How do I teach my children how to have healthy relationships as a single parent?

Single parents have a very difficult job. Not only are they shouldering the weight of caring for their children by being both mother and father most of the time but they also have the responsibility of teaching their children about relationships. We tell the single parents we see in counseling that the best thing that they can do for their children is to become as healthy as they possibly can be. It is not just important to learn about healthy relationships. It is also important to live them out, in front of your children. The hurt and pain of divorce can be devastating for parents. Dealing with this tragedy can cause them to forget about their children. As hard as it is, try to remember that they are suffering too and that you are setting an example of what healthy relationships look like as you date as a single parent.

How does a stepfamily teach ACODPs to beat the odds?

Research shows that some 30 percent of all children spend some portion of their childhood in a stepfamily. This same research also shows that children reared in stepfamilies do not fare as well as children raised in intact families. Since second marriages are at a higher risk for divorce than first marriages, this can also make it difficult to teach children and stepchildren how to have healthy relationships. Seeing these statistics can demoralize stepparents. One of the biggest ways that stepparents can beat the odds against them is to work hard on building and maintaining their relationship. Often, when we see second marriages in counseling, their presenting problem is how to deal with the children and stepchildren. Conflicting over childrearing issues even further erodes the children's knowledge and example of what healthy relationships should look like. We give stepparents some common tips to help strengthen their relationships and set good examples for their children. A sampling of a few of those tips:

- Don't expect everything to be perfect when blending a family. Children have loyalty issues that may get in the way of them being able to really enjoy their stepfamily. Remember, there is no such thing as *The Brady Bunch.* They were a television fantasy, not a real human reality.

- Blending a family can cause you to ignore your marriage.
  Be conscious of this and put special time and energy into your
  marriage.
- Compliment your mate regularly in front of the kids. Take time
  to affirm them in front of the children. This is a good example
  for them.
- Don't expect change to happen all at once. Blending a family
  takes time. Some theorists say it can take up to seven years for
  a family to adjust to blending.
- Have fun and play together as a couple and as a family.
  Establish new rituals and routines through shared activities.
- Find specific ways to relate to your stepchildren. Don't try
  too hard or be too syrupy or fake. Be real and genuine in your
  attempts. Remember, they feel disloyal when they like you,
  so be sensitive to this.
- Respect the uniqueness of your blended family. Be aware that
  you may have to play by a different set of rules than intact
  families. Be adaptable.

If one parent does not want to have contact with the children, how do you teach healthy relationship patterns in this situation?

This is one of the hardest situations to deal with. Some divorced parents, often the father, begin to phase out their relationships with their children after divorce. They may even move away. This leaves the children bereft. It is hard for the remaining parent to teach about healthy relationships to a child who has been wounded so badly. Explaining "father hunger" to your children, both female and male, will help them in dating relationships. Finding ways to help preserve their self-esteem in the midst of this kind of rejection is good as well. Many children of divorce come to our counseling center to deal with this very issue. We help them see the rejection that they are feeling as the fault of their selfish parent, not their own. This is truly a tragedy of divorce.

How can you help your children forgive you for divorcing?

We do not live in a perfect world. Divorce is a consequence of this. Holding a grudge against parents for divorcing is natural for the brokenhearted child. The best thing a parent can do is give the child time.

Guilting and shaming them is destructive. Being defensive about the circumstances of the divorce is counterproductive. Being honest, patient, respectful of their feelings, and expressing genuine sorrow for their grief are very helpful ways to help your child learn to forgive.

How can we help our adult children of divorce beat the odds of divorce in their own marriages?

We tell divorced couples that the best way to help your adult children beat the odds is to be the healthiest person and parent that you can possibly be. Watching your example of health is one of the best models they can have of what is healthy in relationships. Honestly telling them the mistakes you made in your marriage helps them learn what not to do. Helping them find resources and mentors for healthy relationships is also very helpful. The tools and techniques in this book are also excellent resources for ACODPs.

Can ACODPs beat the odds against them?

After reading this book, you now see that the answer is a resounding, *yes*! ACODPs may have to work harder and become aware of their particular issues, but they can indeed beat the odds against them and have happy, healthy, lasting marriages. We are two real-life examples of how this can be a reality.

We have had the privilege in the last twenty-two years to work with quite a few adult children of divorced parents. Many of them came to us for help with their own ailing marriages and did not even know that there was a connection between being an ACODP and being at a high risk for divorce themselves. Some were a little upset at first about being labeled. Some even worried that this labeling might even be a crutch for them and others. We have found that just the opposite has occurred. It is because of the labeling that ACODPs have an identity, a reason for their pain, and an explanation for their behavior. This has brought them a greater understanding and motivation to change. Identifying the specific characteristics of ACODPs has given them reasons, not excuses for their struggles. These reasons are not a crutch but rather a bridge. They bring awareness, and through awareness, hope for change. The following are some comments that these ACODPs wanted to give to you, the reader, about how to beat the odds against you.

Comments

Nancy and Craig have been married for six years. Nancy loves Craig very much, but until she came to counseling, she did not know why she was very suspicious of his motives and always worried that he would leave her. Finding out that these are symptoms of being an ACODP was very freeing for her. Her advice to you is, "Be aware that suspicion and lack of trust are great plagues to the ACODP. They will haunt you in your marriage if you don't deal with them in a healthy way."

Alisha was a college freshman whose parents had had a horrible split when she was in high school. At that time, she also broke up with her boyfriend and has not dated since. Upon hearing us speak at her university, she realized that her fear of dating was a fear of being hurt like her mother was when her parents split after twenty-five years of marriage. This information helped her deal with her trepidation about dating and begin to gain confidence in relationships and marriage. Alisha's advice to single ACODPs is, "Do the work on yourself that you need to do in healing the fear that are holding you back. Be really conscious of the specific issues that trouble ACODPs, such as low self-esteem and the fear of doom. Read and study a lot about healthy relationships, since you don't have a good role model of marriage to follow."

Dave and Mary both came from divorced homes. They came into counseling because they were both suffering from depression and were miserable in their marriage. Helping them become aware of their issues as ACODPs and feel their pain was difficult. They had very poor communications skills, which caused them a great deal of trouble in their marriage. After doing a lot of work, Dave and Mary felt that their marriage had a better chance of being successful. Their advice to ACODPs is, "It is easy to get overwhelmed with marriage and want to give up, like our parents did. Hang in there and learn the skills to communicate in a healthy manner. Doing this saved us from the same fate that befell our parents."

Margie and Stan had been married ten years and had two small children. Stan came from an intact family, but described his parents as being miserable with each other. Margie's parents split when she was two years old. She never even knew her father. Her mom never remarried and raised Margie and her three siblings as a single mom. Margie learned to be strong and do for herself. They came into counseling because Stan had made several bad business decisions and put the family in a very precarious position financially. Margie was so upset with him that she wanted to leave. She did not trust Stan to take care of her.

In counseling she learned that her adaptation to struggles in childhood was to be a strong, in-control person and just do things for herself. This is exactly what she wanted to do in her marriage. Through counseling, they realized that their childhood issues were impacting each other so that interactivity was occurring regularly. This couple learned ways to work together to resolve their problems. Margie's advice to other ACODPs is, "Just because you had to be strong and take care of yourself as a child of divorce doesn't mean that you have to have the same independence and intensity in your marriage. You will have to work harder than most to trust that your partner can take care of you. You will have to learn to break down the walls and share your needs with your partner and learn to trust. It is hard, but it is worth it."

Brian was thirty-eight years old and came into counseling because of a series of failed relationships. His parents divorced when he was twelve years old and constantly played him against each other as a pawn. They were still doing this at the time he came in for counseling. Many of his struggles with relationships were a direct result of his loyalty issues with his parents. Because he always felt guilty and insecure, he would cling to the women he dated for fear that they would find fault with him and leave him. He created his own self-fulfilling prophecy and this is eventually what happened every time.

This insight caused him to confront his parents about what they were doing to him and ask them to stop. While they were terribly defensive and tried to deny the damage they had done, they did back off and this gave Brian the freedom to move forward in his dating relationships. He is now happily married and feels a great deal of confidence that his marriage will last. His advice to ACODPs is, "You have to deal with your unresolved loyalty issues with your parents. Otherwise, you will project them on to your partner. Owning the fear and exorcising it helps you gain the freedom and confidence you need to choose a lifetime partner. This is the best piece of work that I have ever done. It helped me find my beautiful wife. I would strongly encourage every ACODP to do this work."

Cathy was an ACODP in her second marriage to Glen, whose parents were still married after thirty-five years. Cathy and Glen were trying to blend a family with her two children and his two sons. They came into marriage counseling because they were on the verge of another divorce. They were at odds about the children and could not resolve their conflicts. As Cathy explored the pain of her parents' divorce, she realized that she was trying too hard to make everything in her blended family perfect and equitable. This was because the blended family that she lived in as a child was not fair or impartial. The pressure of her previously failed marriage was also weighting on her greatly. Cathy felt so much stress that she had to succeed, that she was constantly on guard. Her state of unremitting vigilance caused her husband and children to revolt against her. This just made her control all the more. This power struggle was killing their marriage.

In counseling, Cathy saw how deeply hurt she was about her parents' divorce and her father having another family. She felt constant rejection and that she was taking second place to his new children. She vowed to herself that her children would never have to suffer like this, so when she married Glen, she was going to see to it that everything was fair, equitable, and perfect. This was an impossible task and was indeed destroying Cathy as well as her marriage. She learned that she did not have to work so hard to protect her children or make things fair, that in blended families fair is relative and can seldom be achieved. She further learned that the best thing she could do for herself and her family was deal with the pain of her childhood so she could be free from the curse of perfection. She did the hard work of accomplishing this task. Unloading this burden made her the happy, peaceful woman that Glen fell in love with. As Cathy relaxed and did not worry so much, she and Glen could communicate better. They learned some of the conflict resolution skills we teach ACODPs and began to solve some of the differences they had with the children.

Resolving the issues of her parents' divorce and purging herself of the guilt of her first divorce gave Cathy the emotional energy to loosen up and enjoy the new family she and Glen blended together. Cathy's advice to ACODPs is, "Make sure you deal with your childhood wounds of rejection and pain around your parents' divorce, because they will surely come back to bite you if you don't. If you are divorced, let your children process their issues about it, but don't feel so guilty and responsible that you try to make everything perfect. This is an impossible task and will not work. It will harm your family, rather than helping it. Don't try to make your blended family fair or equitable. This is not possible. Each child has another parent who can mess up your equitable balance. Just try to deal with your own stuff, forgive yourself, and love the family you have now. This will help you and your spouse better resolve conflicts and reconcile differences."

These are just a few of the ACODPs that we have treated over the past twenty-two years who wanted to share with you how they beat the odds against them. There were many more, but space would not allow them a chance to share. We hope their sharing was as inspiring for you as it was for us.

Epilogue

If you have read to this point you have made an amazing journey with us while we have told our stories as two adult children of divorced parents who have found ways to make our marriage work for twenty-five years. We have struggled and survived, and in some areas, have conquered the demons that plague ACODPs. We began our journey with awareness that we had issues that haunted us which would not seem to abate. With further exploration and study, we learned that many adult children of divorced parents struggle with the same issues. This awareness gave words to our pain and helped us see that not only are we not alone but that by knowing the core of our relational problems, we have a better chance of healing. This process put us on the road to feeling our pain. Feeling the pain of our parents' divorces was difficult for us. We followed the adage we use in therapy that says, "First we hurt, then we feel, next we heal." This led us to the realization that we were wounded in the areas of trust, fear, insecurity, and communication, and that we needed marital mentors as an example to follow. To deal with these wounds we developed exercises, tools, and techniques that helped us beat the odds against us. We learned early in our marriage that communication, empathy, and forgiveness were essential ingredients in preserving our marriage and ourselves.

Here we are today, after twenty-five years of marriage, and after an equal amount of time dealing with our own issues that have impacted our marriage, realizing that we have come full circle. We have learned how to face our fears and the wounds that have impacted our souls and we have also learned how to resolve them. Many of our insecurities as ACODPs have been dealt with. Some still rear their ugly heads, but we have an arsenal of communication weapons to combat them. These tools have saved our marriage and now we can, with confidence, teach them to you.

As we have done all through this manuscript, we wanted to end where we began, by sharing the conclusions of our stories with you.

Bev's Story

When I walk into my home, on a table in the front foyer is a beautiful silver urn. It shines so brightly that those who enter often comment on it. The story of this urn is illustrative of my life.

When I was a young girl my sister and I would play for hours outside. One of our favorite things to do was to make mud pies. One sunny day we found a pot in our makeshift, dirty garage. It was a tarnished, brown ugly-looking pot, so we were sure it would be all right to play with it. We served ourselves creative, handcrafted mud dishes in this pot pretending that they were delicious delicacies and exotic cuisine. Pretending was always a great escape from the pain of our childhood. The problem with pretending was that I did not know when to stop. Even in adulthood I pretended that I did not feel the pain of my family's dissolution.

One day while we were playing my mother came out and scolded us for playing with this pot. "Don't put mud and dirt in there!" she cried. "This is a valuable urn." "What?" We shrieked incredulously! "How could this old pot be valuable? Look at it. It's brown and dingy and dirty." Nevertheless, she grabbed the pot and took it inside. Several days later, we saw the pot on the windowsill and grabbed it when my mom was not looking. What joy it was to restore it to its rightful purpose, serving mud pies for impish children. For several years the struggle went on. We would get scolded for using the pot and Mom would take it inside. We would sneak it outside and use it again and so the cycle went. Eventually, we gave up our mud pie phase. After that the ugly pot sat on the windowsill in the hot sun looking very unsightly. It stayed there for years and was ultimately tossed in the makeshift garage into a junk pile.

I remember seeing the pot the day that I left my home for good. As I said earlier, my relationship with my mother suffered after I left. She forbade me to come home after I went to live with my father. Several years passed and she softened and extended an invitation for me to visit. Those few visits were difficult because she was bitter, angry, and resentful.

In due course, our relationship faded. I could not take the craziness, anger, and negativity, and she could not tolerate a daughter that wanted health. For my own sanity I had to withdraw from her. Except for her outrage at my disrespect, she hardly noticed. During that time I prayed, meditated, completed graduate school, went to therapy, studied what healthy families were like, and eventually created one of my own; one without craziness; one with love and commitment.

I flourished in my newly created family and began to heal from the pain that I experienced as a child. One thing that I held onto was that Tom and I had a made a commitment and we were going to honor it. There were no back doors for us. Like Thornton Wilder's character Mrs. Antrobus in his play *The Skin of Our Teeth,* I said to my husband, "I did not marry you because you were perfect. I married you because you gave me a promise. This promise made up for your faults and the promise I gave you made up for mine. Two imperfect people got married, and it was the promise that made it a marriage." In the promise of my marriage I found healing for the dissolution of my own nuclear family.

Fifteen years later I received a call from a relative. My mother had dropped dead of an aneurysm. No one was there by her side. How tragic that she had alienated all of her family, so much so that no one was there when she breathed her last breath. Divorce indeed dissolves families.

A year later, I went to the house to clean up her meager belongings and sell the pitiful, pathetic place. As I was going through her paltry possessions I came across the pot. I kept very few of her things: a photo, a teacup, a scarf, and that dirty old pot. I then said goodbye to the house that held so many painful memories for me.

Back home, I unpacked the small box of things. I spied the pot. As I pulled it out, I could not help but think about what my mother had said so many years ago. Was this indeed a valuable urn? Could anything so ugly be so valuable? My curiosity got the best of me and I drug out all of the cleaners and metal polishers that I could find. I scrubbed and scoured and rubbed in vain. Finally, I pulled out the big guns, the super silver polish. The pot was so damaged that I finally just immersed it in a vat of pure liquid silver polish. What happened next was astonishing. To my amazement, the ugly old pot was transformed into a beautiful silver urn. The sparkle was so dazzling that it took my breath away. Tears filled my eyes and I began to weep. For a moment, I thought that I was losing it. I couldn't figure out why I was moved to such emotion. Was it because I was beholding the last remnant of the family I once knew? Was it due to the fact that I was reliving my painful childhood? No, I think it was because I realized the similarities between me and that dingy, dark pot.

After the demise of my family I spent most of my life feeling dingy and dark inside. So much of that time I felt like I was not valuable. With hard cleansing work and many applications of healing agents such as prayer, meditation, therapy, education, and skills training, my life and my marriage began to sparkle. My marriage and my life could have been the ugly brown pot but with diligence, work, and faith, it has become a beautiful silver urn that I will cherish.

Tom's Story

I had spent the first fifteen years of our marriage dealing with and resolving the issues around my parents' divorce and how they impacted me and harmed my marriage. I had even done a great deal of work in dealing with my own pain and resultant anger, and somewhat restored my relationships with both of my parents. The only lingering effect of being an ACODP for me was the lack of affirmation and validation that I needed so much from my father.

I was doing some powerful work personally in terms of feeling loved and affirmed, even without my father's affirmation, and coincidentally at that time, he happened to call and invite us to a reunion for his side of the family. I would be visiting with relatives that I had not seen for more than twenty years, a direct result of my parents' divorce. Needless to say, I had some fear and trepidation about going, but was equally convinced that I needed to go, if for no other reason than to exorcise the demons of my past.

With much prayer and planning we set out on our trek of hoped-for healing with dad and his family. I worked hard to love and affirm myself, in preparation for the trip. I felt remarkably loveable and affirmed as we went. We met my father and his wife at the airport in Los Angeles and immediately drove with them to the family reunion in Central California. I later reflected that it was a remarkable trip because all of the members of my dad's family received me in love. I found myself in a circle of my aunts and uncles and cousins whom I had not seen for two decades. We shared and talked and laughed, and I have to say that I was as lovable as I could be. Then, I shared with my sweet Portuguese grandmother whom I had missed for so long. I noticed however, that every circle that I was in all day long, my father was not in there with me. In fact, he was in circles opposite of me for the whole day.

The day wore on and we prepared to leave. We came to the inevitable time when we had to say good-bye to everyone. I began to embrace each one, and again to my surprise, my father was on the opposite side of the circle saying his good-byes as well. Honestly at that point, I felt that I had been as lovable as I could be. My thought was to briefly say good-bye to my father, hug him, and leave as quickly as possible. In that moment I found that I did not want to risk not being affirmed again. As I approached my father, I reached out to hug him and pull away. But I noticed as I began to pull away, that something very strange happened. The more I pulled away, the more he pulled me closer. I remember feeling self-conscious initially about two grown men hugging each other in public. But that feeling promptly dissipated as I suddenly felt like I was no longer a grown man; I was a little boy who was melting into his daddy's arms. As we stood there hugging each other, my dad then did the strangest thing. He kissed me on the cheek and whispered into my ear how much he loved me and how proud he was of me. I was stunned. I can still hear those words ringing in my ears. It was what I had wanted to hear all of my life, but couldn't because of the unresolved issues around my parents' divorce.

For a few brief seconds I stood there speechless. We all then wiped away our tears and left. Bev, the girls, and I proceeded to get into the car. There was a stunned silence in the car that lasted for almost an hour. Finally, I turned to Bev and stuttered, "Did you see what happened back there?" I was still reeling in disbelief. She hesitantly responded, "Yes, I did see." "Why did that happen?" I questioned. "Why, after all of these years, did dad finally give me what I desperately needed?" Thoughtfully Bev said, "I think it was because you believed that you were lovable whether dad affirmed you or not. Since you loved yourself, it gave him the freedom to be loving to you as well. Maybe you are healing those childhood wounds of divorce after all."

I thought about that for a while and realized that there was hope for us as ACODPs. We really can do the work and feel the pain and heal the wounds of our parents' divorces, if we are willing to. We, as ACODPs, can beat the odds against us and live healthy, happy lives in lasting, fulfilling marriages.

Bibliography

Bowen, Murray. *Family Therapy in Clinical Practice*. New York: Jason Aronson, 1978.

Fagan, Patrick, and Robert Rector. "The Effects of Divorce on America." *The Heritage Foundation Backgrounder Newsletter* (June 5, 2000).

Gottman, John. *The Marriage Clinic: A Scientifically Based Marital Therapy*. New York: W.W. Norton, 1999.

Helms, Ann Doss. "For the Kids' Sake." *The Charlotte Observer* (2 January 2001): sec. D, 1–2.

Hendrix, Harville. *Getting the Love You Want*. New York: Harper Perennial, 1990.

Hendrix, Harville. *Keeping the Love You Find*. New York: Pocket Books, 1992.

Lauer, Jeanette and Robert. "Marriages Made to Last." *Psychology Today* 19, no. 6 (June 1985): 85–89.

Lewis, Robert. *Raising a Modern-Day Knight*. Colorado Springs: Focus on the Family Publications, 1998.

Love, Patricia. *The Emotional Incest Syndrome: When a Parent's Love Rules Your Life*. New York: Bantam,1990.

Marquardt, Elizabeth. "Children of Divorce: Stories of Exile." *The Christian Century* (February 2001): 24–27.

Ornstein, Robert, and David Sobel. *The Healing Brain*. New York: Simon and Schuster, 1987.

Rodgers, Beverly and Tom. *How to Find Mr. or Ms. Right: A Practical Guide to Finding a Soul Mate*. San Jose, Calif.: Resource Publications, Inc., 1999.

———. *Soul-Healing Love: Ten Practical, Easy-to-Learn Techniques for Couples in Crisis*. San Jose, Calif.: Resource Publications, Inc., 1998.

Smedes, Lewis. *Forgive and Forget: Healing the Hurts We Don't Deserve*. San Francisco: Harper and Row, 1984.

Waite, Linda, and Maggie Gallagher. *The Case for Marriage: Why Married People Are Happier, Healthier, and Better Off Financially*. New York: Doubleday, 2000.

Wallerstein, Judith; Julia Lewis; and Sandra Blakeslee. *The Unexpected Legacy of Divorce.* New York: Hyperion, 2000.